ABOUT THE AUTHOR

Bill Tidy was born in Preston in 1933, and moved to Liverpool in 1940 in time for the Blitz – which he survived. He also survived the obligatory office-boy job in a shipping office, and later a three-year stint with the army in Germany, Korea, and Japan where his first cartoon appeared in a Japanese newspaper. On leaving the army he joined a Liverpool advertising agency, and took up cartooning in 1957.

The Fosdyke Sagas have become comic classics; he has recently embarked on writing for children; and 'The Great Eric Ackroyd Disaster' was staged as a musical at the Oldham Coliseum. Bill Tidy also contributes to *Punch*, *Private Eye*, the *Daily Mirror*, BBC, ITV, advertising agencies, and everyone else. He received the Granada TV 'What the Papers Say' award for Cartoonist of the Year in 1974, and the Society of Strip Illustrations award in 1980.

His wife is a Neapolitan, and they have three children.

By Bill Tidy
and published by New English Library:

BILL TIDY'S LITTLE RUDE BOOK
BILL TIDY'S BOOK OF CLASSIC COCK-UPS

BILL TIDY'S BOOK OF CLASSIC COCK-UPS

Bill Tidy drew the pictures
Graham Nown wrote the
stories

NEW ENGLISH LIBRARY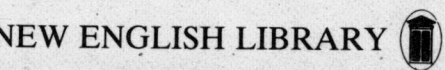

A New English Library Original Publication 1985

First NEL Paperback Edition November 1985

NEL Books are published by
New English Library,
Mill Road, Dunton Green,
Sevenoaks, Kent.
Editorial office: 47 Bedford Square, London WC1B 3DP

Typeset by Rowland Phototypesetting Ltd,
Bury St Edmunds, Suffolk.
Printed and bound by
Cox & Wyman Ltd, Reading, Berks.

British Library C.I.P.

Tidy, Bill
    Bill Tidy's book of classic cock-ups
    I. Title   II. Nown, Graham
    741.5'942   PN6737.T5

    ISBN 0 450 05894 8

BILL TIDY'S BOOK OF CLASSIC COCK-UPS

FORE!

Life is one long banana-skin. If you have your doubts just spare a thought for the unfortunates who skid across the following pages.

Those of us who have blundered into embarrassing situations and emerged battered, boozed, bankrupt or bruised will know that the fascination in these little stories does not lie in laughing at someone's downfall. It's that we have all been there ourselves.

Who can't feel a curious kinship with the BBC presenter who solemnly announced: 'This is the British Broadcorping Castration'? Or the US highway patrolman who hit another car head-on and leapt from the wreckage and booked himself?

Thanks to the diligent cock-up chroniclers of our national newspapers and magazines, and the inspiration of fellow collectors Richard Smith, Edward Decter and Bill Bryson Jr.

Mind how you go!

Bill Tidy
May 1985

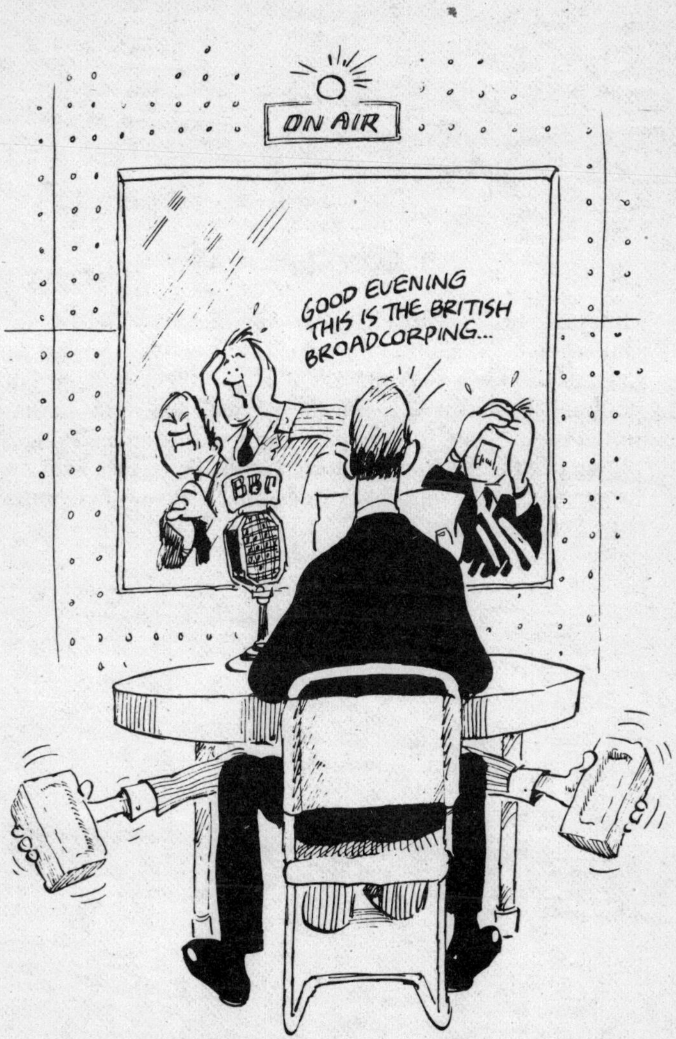
ON AIR
BBC
GOOD EVENING
THIS IS THE BRITISH
BROADCORPING...

THE LONG GOODBYE

American tourist Clive Kluys could not see enough of Rio. But when he looked at his watch he realised with horror that his ship was leaving. Clive arrived breathless at Rio de Janeiro dockside to see it pulling away. He made a tremendous leap for the deck, missed completely, and plunged into the murky water. When they fished him out he discovered it was the wrong ship. The one he wanted sailed an hour later.

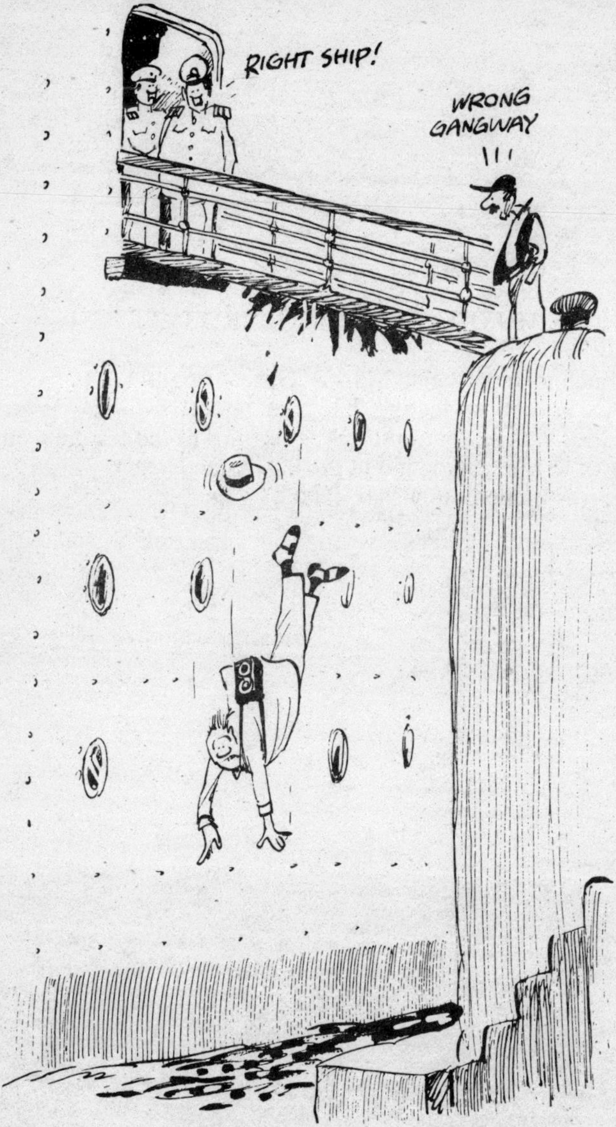
RIGHT SHIP!
WRONG GANGWAY

THE MOST CONVINCING BIRD IMPRESSION

French ornithologist Marius Giraud spent hours in his living room perfecting his bird impersonations. When Marius was ready to put his repertoire to the test he went down to the woods, hid in the bushes and began whistling. He was immediately shot dead by a hunter.

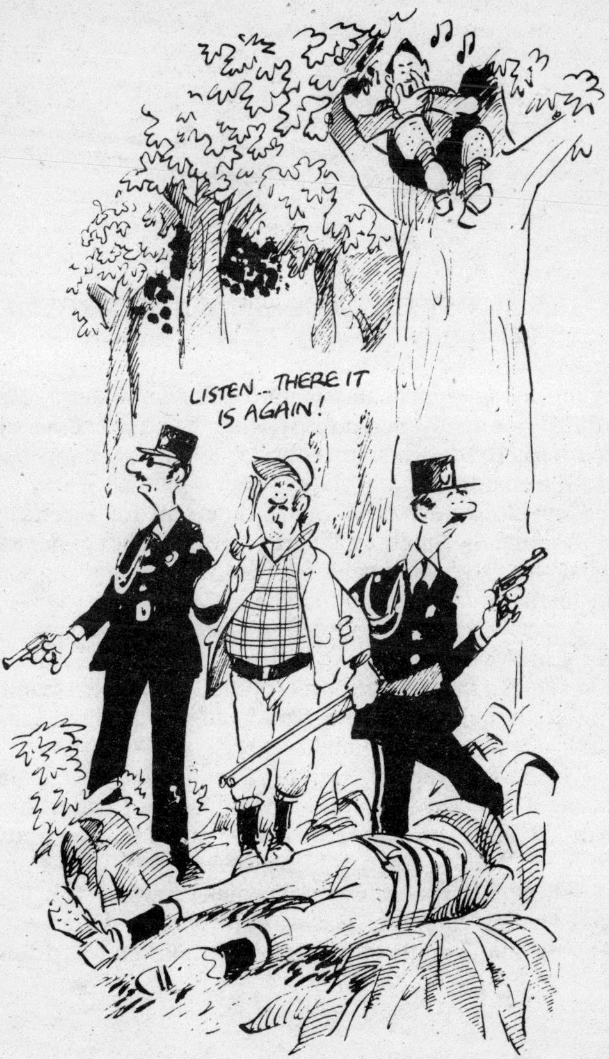
LISTEN... THERE IT IS AGAIN!

THE MOST UNSUCCESSFUL ATTEMPT TO COMMUNICATE WITH A FOREIGNER

When his load went missing a foreign lorry driver made straight for the nearest police station. But try as they could, the baffled Birmingham bobbies could not make out a word he said.

Convinced he was German, they sent for a colleague who spoke the language fluently. He could not understand what the driver was babbling about either and suggested he might be Latvian – or maybe Icelandic.

A growing number of bobbies, all anxious to help, sent for a professor who spoke Icelandic. But he drew a blank too. Then a Latvian interpreter rolled up. He was stumped but he thought the driver, who had been drinking heavily to drown his sorrows, might be Russian.

The police, who were getting a little fed up by this time, brought in a Russian expert. He could not understand a word. Finally the exasperated trucker sobered up enough to bawl: 'Look – I'm a ****ing Geordie.'

When the speechless policemen cracked the heavy accent they found he wasn't even a lorry driver either. He had made up the whole story because he was drunk.

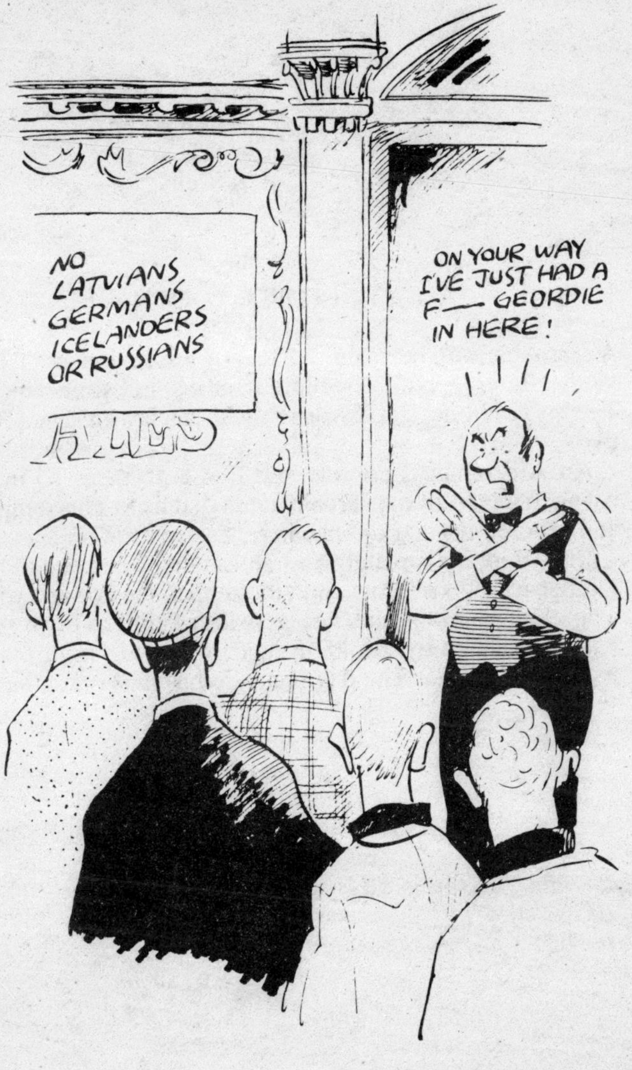
NO
LATVIANS
GERMANS
ICELANDERS
OR RUSSIANS
ON YOUR WAY
I'VE JUST HAD A
F— GEORDIE
IN HERE!

A TOOTH FOR A TOOTH

A storm blew up between coastguard John Tupper and his mother-in-law. And it erupted into a full-scale row – Tupper could not get a word in with his fast-talking relative.

An Australian court was told that he became so irate trying to interrupt the verbal stream that he lost his temper and ordered his dog to seize her.

But Tupper completely underestimated the speed of his mother-in-law's reflexes. She sidestepped the dog and with a lightning reaction sank her teeth into Tupper's thigh. He had to be taken to hospital for treatment. His mother-in-law was fined £25. The dog recovered from shock.

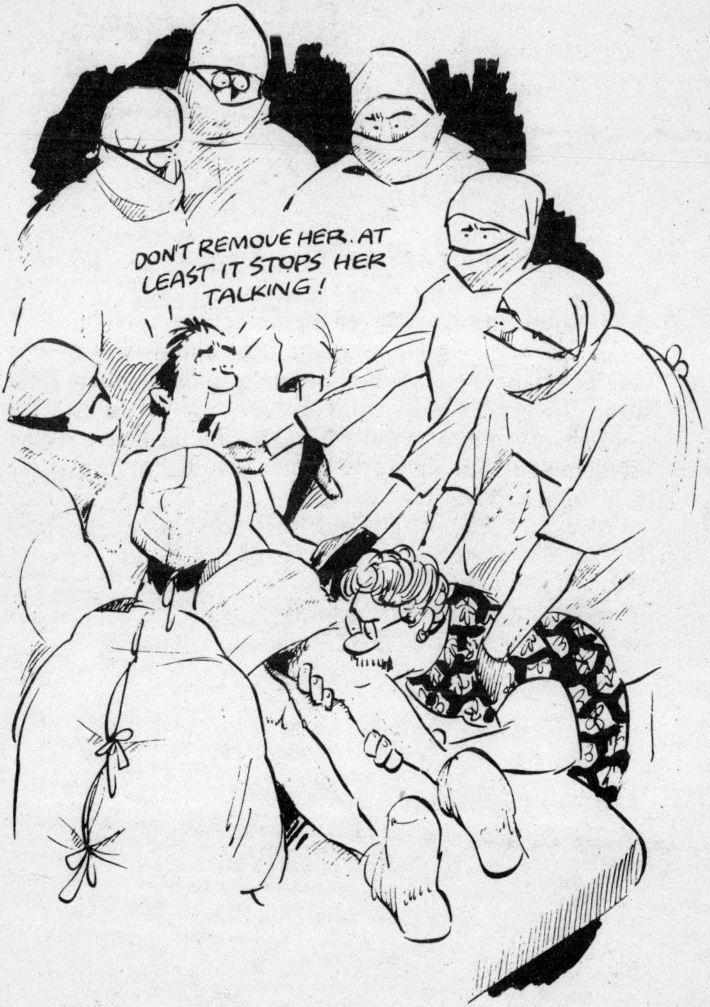
DON'T REMOVE HER. AT LEAST IT STOPS HER TALKING!

THE MOST DISASTROUS TEA-BREAK

A hundred and forty-seven passengers were injured in a rail crash during Chinese National Safety Week. The accident happened when a sweating railway repair gang stopped work to buy ice lollies. As they licked away, a train ploughed into tools they had left on the line, sending accident statistics higher than they were before the safety campaign started.

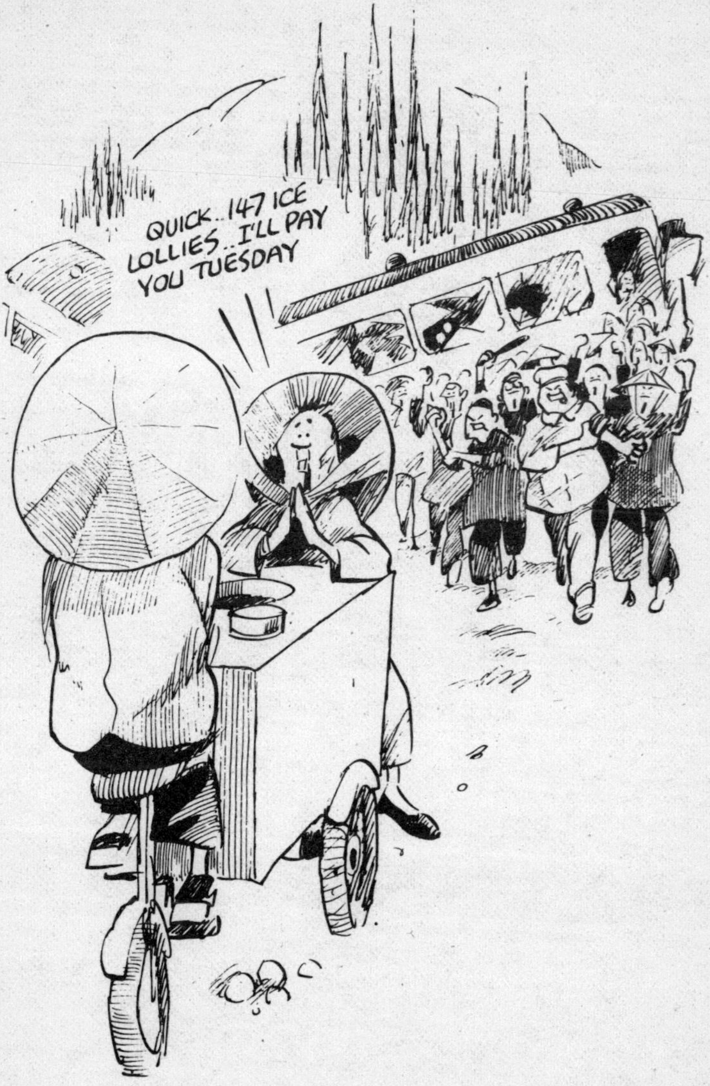
QUICK...147 ICE LOLLIES...I'LL PAY YOU TUESDAY

THE MOST UNSUCCESSFUL ATTEMPT TO READ A NEWSPAPER

A man in Stockport walked downstairs one morning to pick up his morning newspaper from the letterbox.

Later, rather shaken, he reported to police that as he pulled it out a hand appeared through the letter box and pulled two rings from his fingers. The paper was also taken.

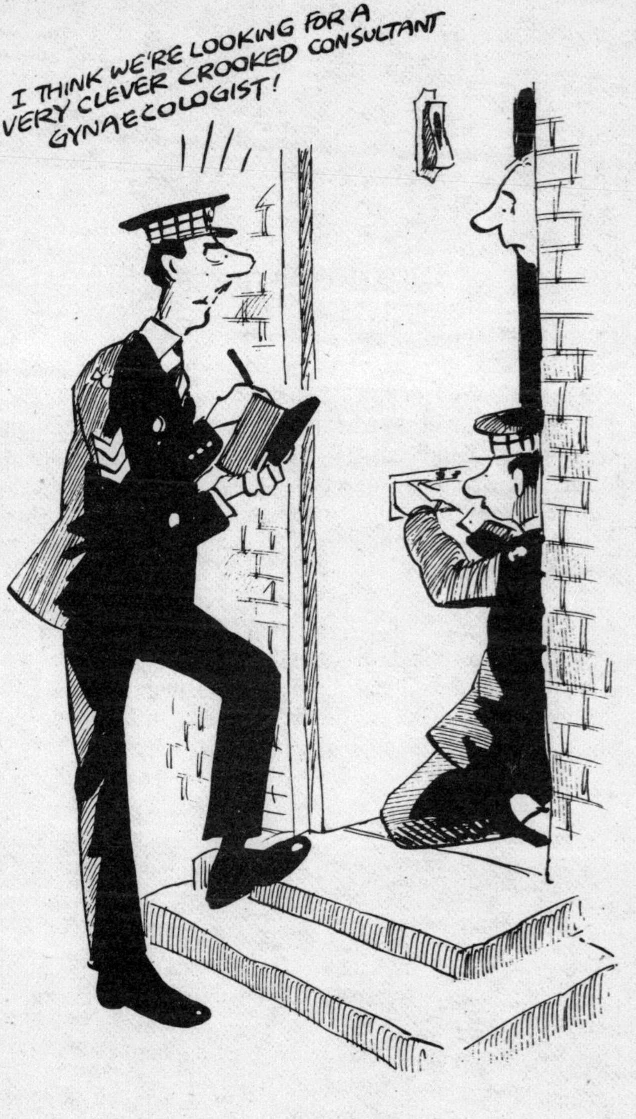
I THINK WE'RE LOOKING FOR A VERY CLEVER CROOKED CONSULTANT GYNAECOLOGIST!

GORDON BENNETT!

In the last century manners were everything. And few were better endowed with the social graces than wealthy socialite James Gordon Bennett.

He was engaged to Caroline May whose well-connected Washington family insisted on decorum carried out to the letter. Which only served to leave them all the more stunned when their future son-in-law strode purposefully into their drawingroom one day, unbuttoned his flies and peed on the fire.

The wedding was cancelled, of course, Caroline May was locked out of his sight and James Gordon Bennett crept away to self-imposed exile in France.

No one believed his story that he had arrived rather the worse for drink, vaguely glimpsed the fireplace and mistaken it for the lavatory.

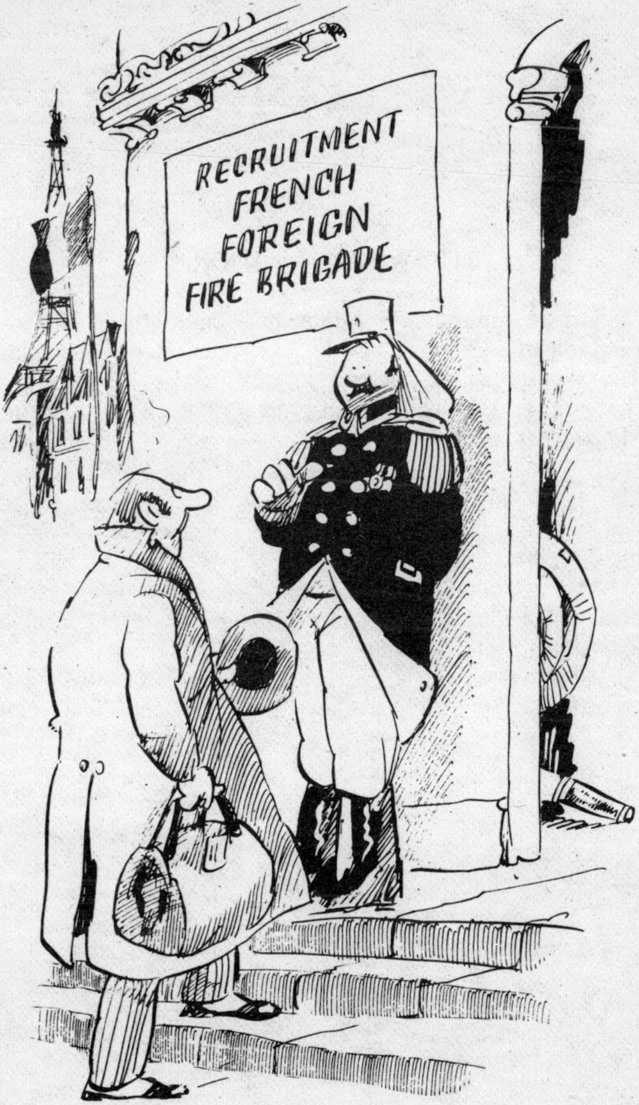
RECRUITMENT
FRENCH
FOREIGN
FIRE BRIGADE

THE WIND OF CHANGE

Optimistic American Gerald Franz, 56, boldly set sail for England in a canoe towed by five kites. But once under way Gerald found himself in dire straits. The breeze changed and blew him all the way back to Boston, Massachusetts.

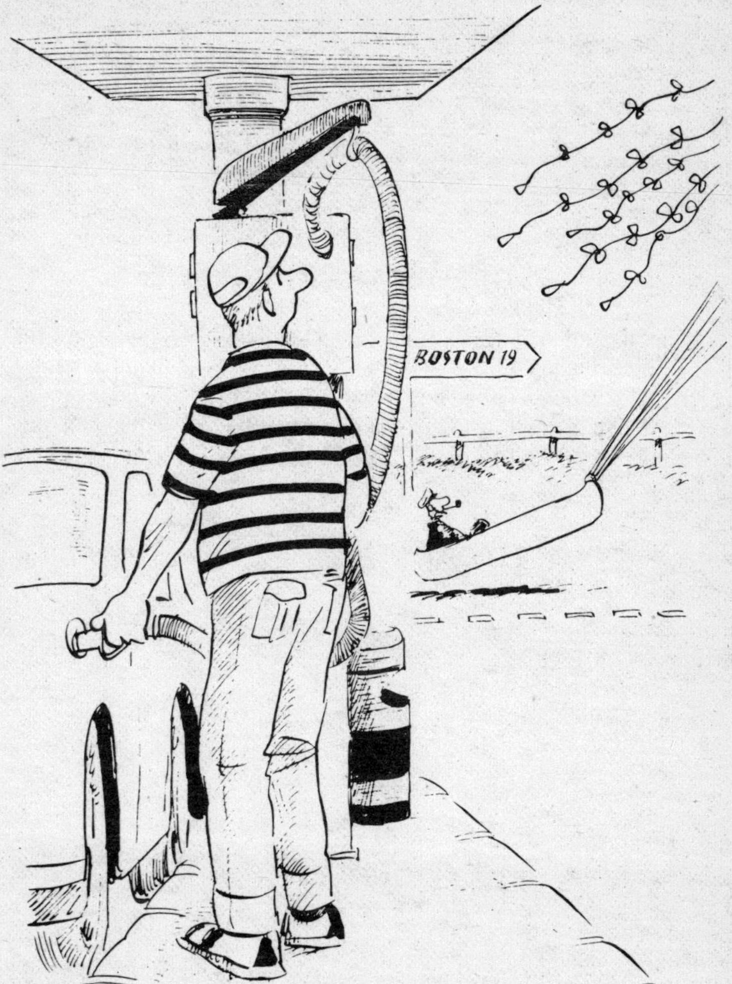
BOSTON 19

THE FIZZ THAT WENT FLAT

Puzzled American advertising executives could not understand why Pepsi was not an instant success in certain parts
of Europe. Then they discovered that their slogan, 'Come
Alive With Pepsi', translated into Slavic as 'Pepsi Brings
Your Ancestors Back From The Grave'.

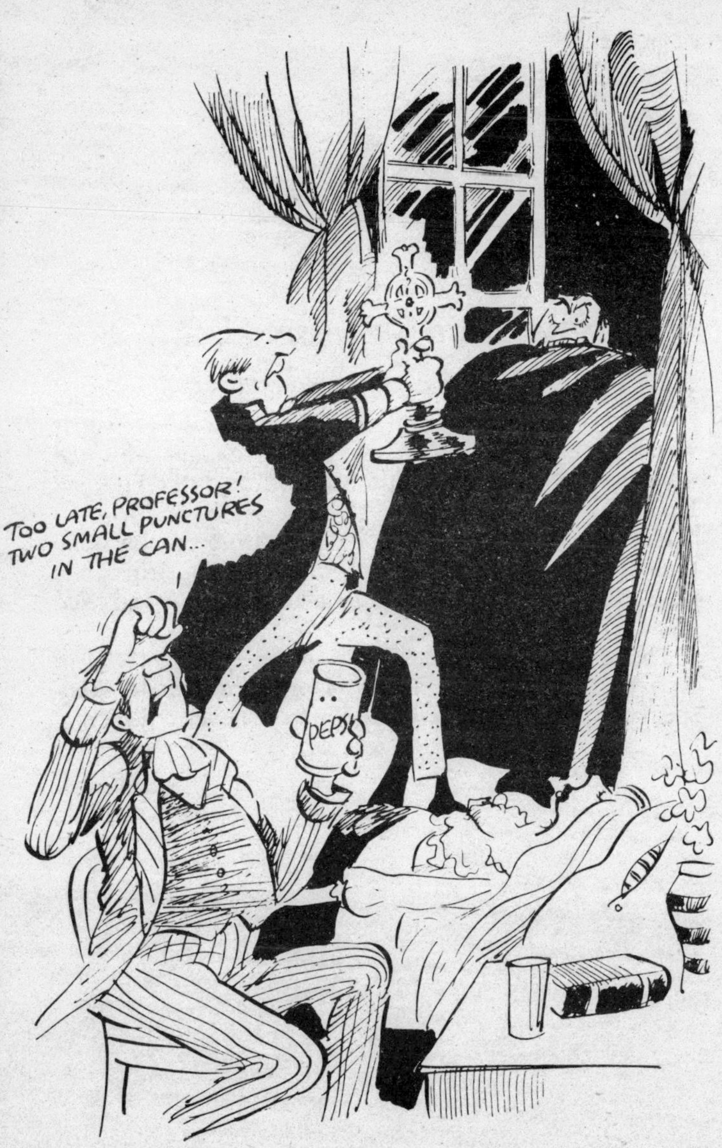
TOO LATE, PROFESSOR! TWO SMALL PUNCTURES IN THE CAN...
PEPSI

THE TAIL OF THE MISSING SHIRTS

When the final whistle blew, Crewe Alexandra soccer team peeled off their shirts and tossed them into the crowd. It was a generous end-of-season gesture to fans who had followed their fortune right to the bottom of the Football League.

But horrified club officials watching from the touchline realised that they could not afford to lose the strip. They plunged into the throng of 1226 astonished fans and tried to snatch them back again.

The club, which was £70,000 in the red, managed to recover them all except two. Despite desperate loud-speaker appeals to the crowd they were never returned.

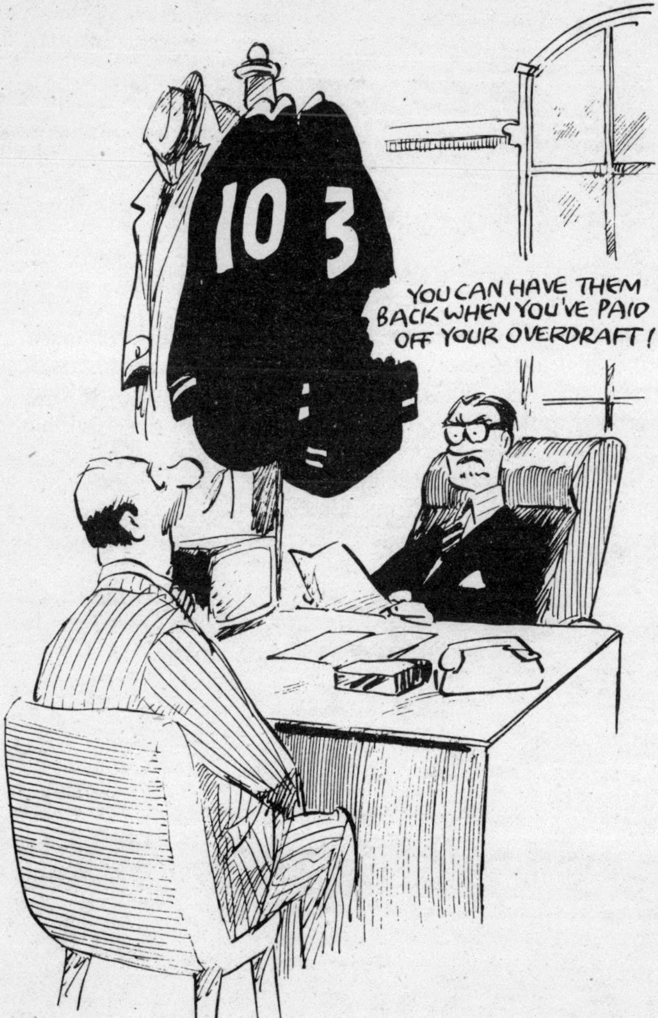
10 3
YOU CAN HAVE THEM BACK WHEN YOU'VE PAID OFF YOUR OVERDRAFT!

I AM FROM BARCELONA . . .

A Spanish prison warder made up his mind to kill himself but just could not make a decent job of it. He shot himself five times point-blank in the chest but each shot missed the vital spot.

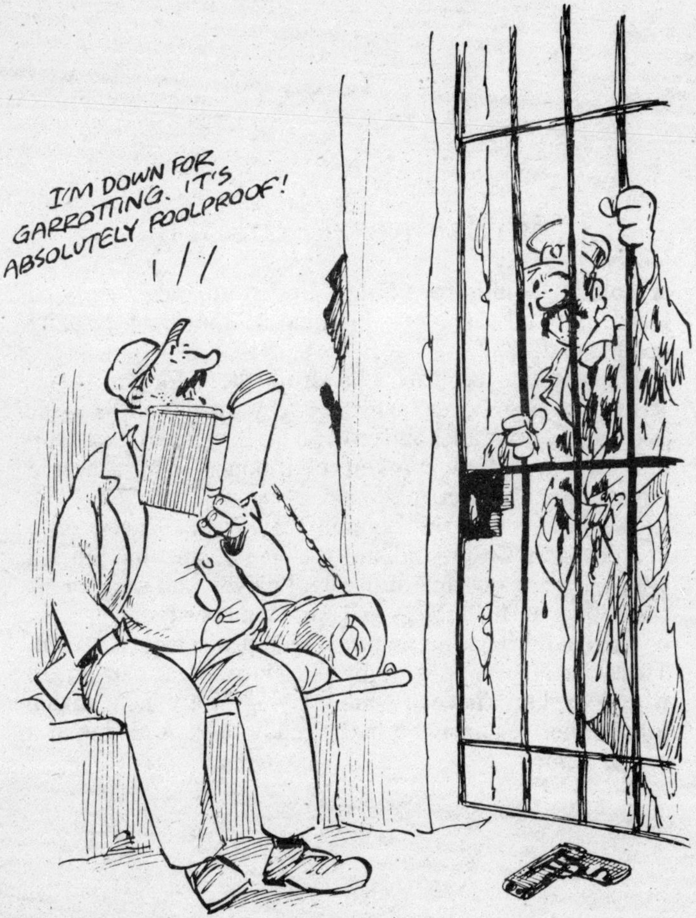
I'M DOWN FOR GARROTTING. IT'S ABSOLUTELY FOOLPROOF!

THE PUB THAT WOULD NOT DIE

A pub in Goldthorpe, South Yorkshire, might be well advised to take a block booking at the local casualty department.

The sporting regulars who drink there formed themselves into five soccer teams, a rugby squad and sides for pool, darts, dominoes and crib. So far they have clocked up four broken legs, two broken collar bones, four dislocated fingers and a broken ankle.

Then there was the domino player who leaned on a lighted cigar while studying the game, and burned his elbow. To say nothing of the pool player who slapped his cash down on the table – and sprained his wrist.

The landlord has his own coveted Special Injury Award. This year it went to a rugby player who was carried off with a broken kneecap while playing in a benefit match for another regular who had already broken his leg in a soccer game.

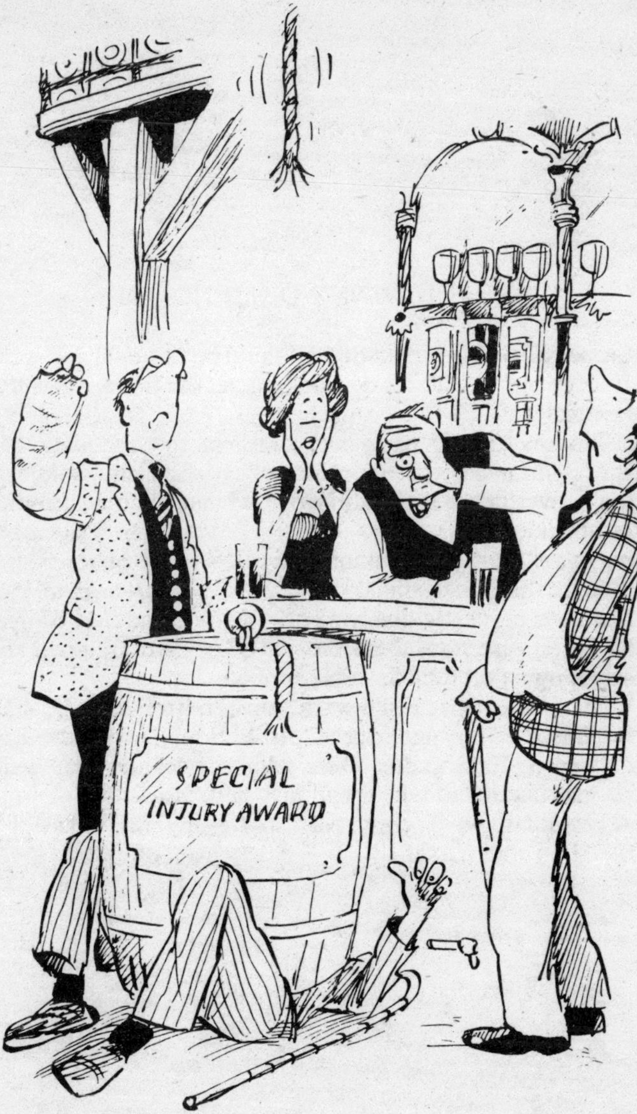
SPECIAL
INJURY AWARD

THE LONE SENTINEL

Lionel Burleigh had waited a long time for February 6th, 1965. It was the day his new newspaper the *Commonwealth Sentinel* was due to be launched.

Months of hard work had gone into the first issue. Mr Burleigh had written most of it himself, sold all the advertising singlehanded and made the printing arrangements.

On the great day his phone rang. It was the police asking if he was the man behind the *Commonwealth Sentinel*. Mr Burleigh modestly admitted that he was indeed. 'Why?' he asked. 'Because there are 50,000 of them blocking the street outside,' the constable replied.

Mr Burleigh realised with some horror that he had organised everything except distribution. The printer had delivered all the copies to his address because there were no instructions to take them anywhere else.

Eventually one copy was sold – by Mr Burleigh's daughter to a passer-by.

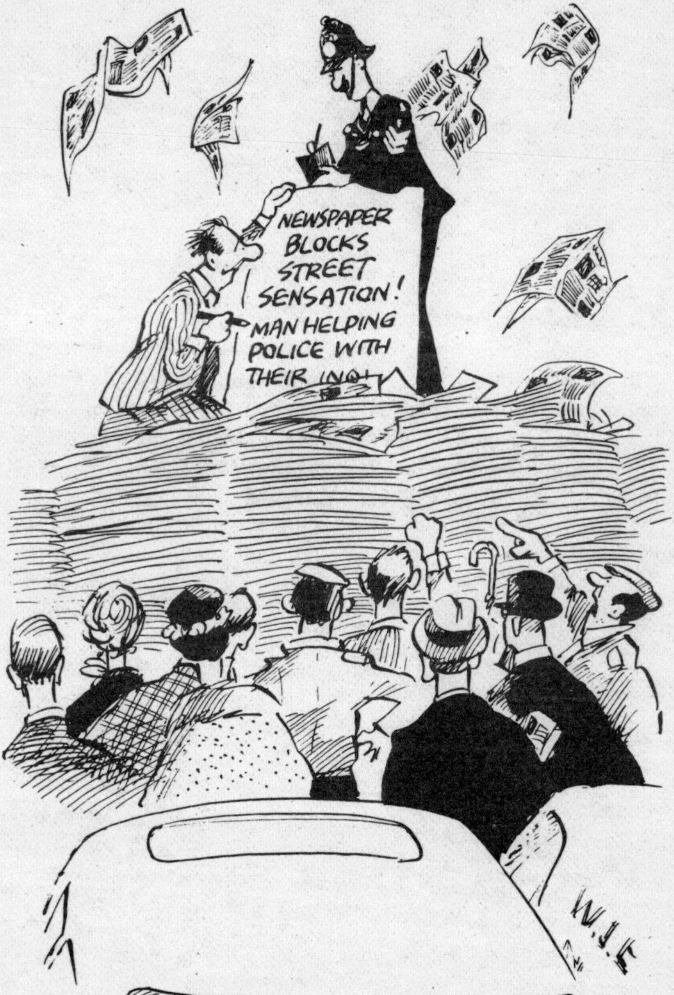
NEWSPAPER BLOCKS STREET SENSATION! MAN HELPING POLICE WITH THEIR INQ
W.J.F.

THE TON-UP TRICKSTER

The Mayor of Toulon, France, threw a lavish civic reception to celebrate bubbly Avril Charbon's 100th birthday. But there were red faces all round when one of the guests recognised her – from an identical reception the year before in Marseilles. Avril confessed that she was really eighty-eight but loved parties so much that she had claimed to be a centenarian eighteen times in six years.

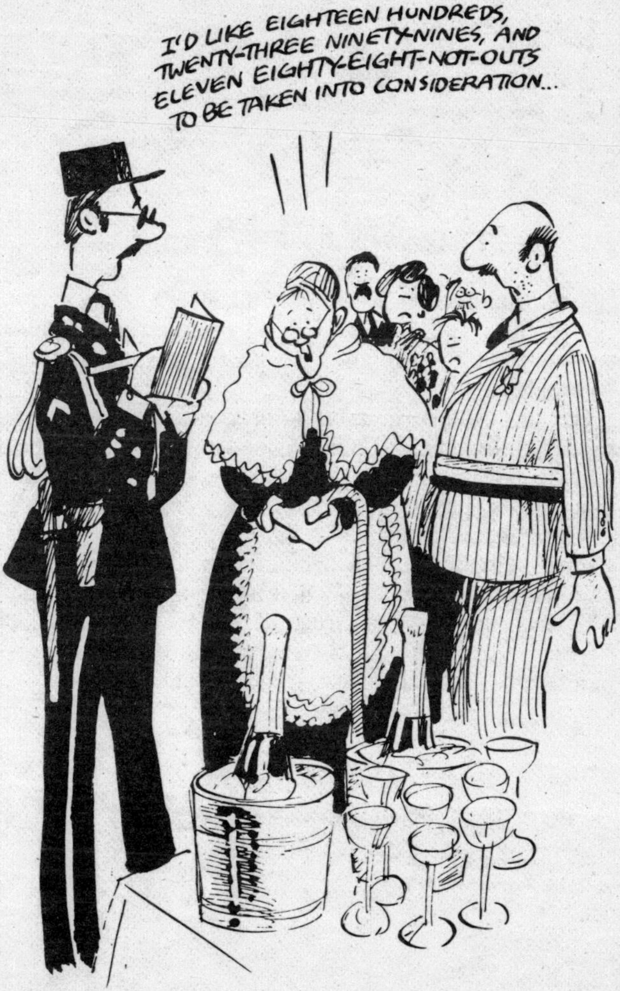
I'D LIKE EIGHTEEN HUNDREDS, TWENTY-THREE NINETY-NINES, AND ELEVEN EIGHTY-EIGHT-NOT-OUTS TO BE TAKEN INTO CONSIDERATION...

BRITAIN'S SECRET WEAPON

Enemy submarines were an unexpected menace during World War I. Sonar and depth-charges had not been invented and the threat to British shipping clearly had to be tackled.

But with the formidable military mind of Admiral Sir Frederick Inglefield, England need not have trembled. He quickly assessed the situation and reached the conclusion that without periscopes submarines were all at sea.

The Admiral's plan was brilliantly simple. Squads of strong swimmers, each armed with a black bag and a hammer, would be despatched to engage the enemy subs.

Their orders were to thrust the bag over the first peeping periscope in sight and then whack it violently with the hammer to crack the glass. It didn't catch on.

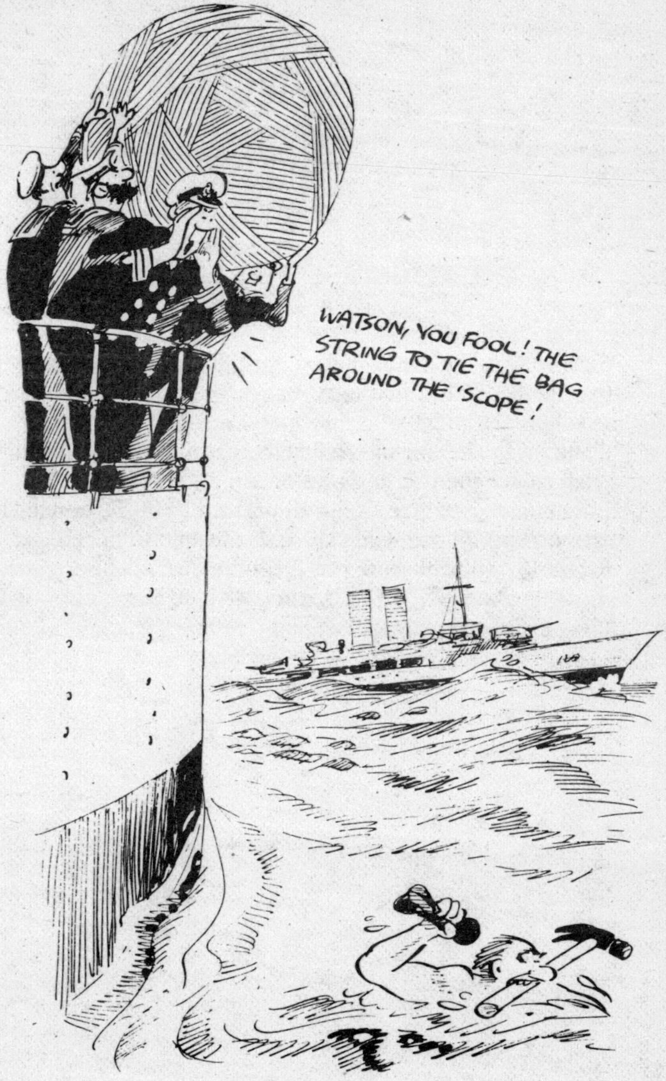
WATSON, YOU FOOL! THE STRING TO TIE THE BAG AROUND THE 'SCOPE!

THE FIRECREW WHO LOOKED TO
THEIR LAURELS

Firemen at the station next to the Stan Laurel pub got themselves into a fine mess.

When they received an emergency call they had to ask drinkers in the bar at Ulverston, Cumbria, to give them a push to get the fire engine started.

The scene, worthy of a Laurel and Hardy movie, had cropped up before when the firecrew had to ask passers-by for help. It took ten pub regulars to get the machine moving. And when the brigade arrived they found it was a false alarm.

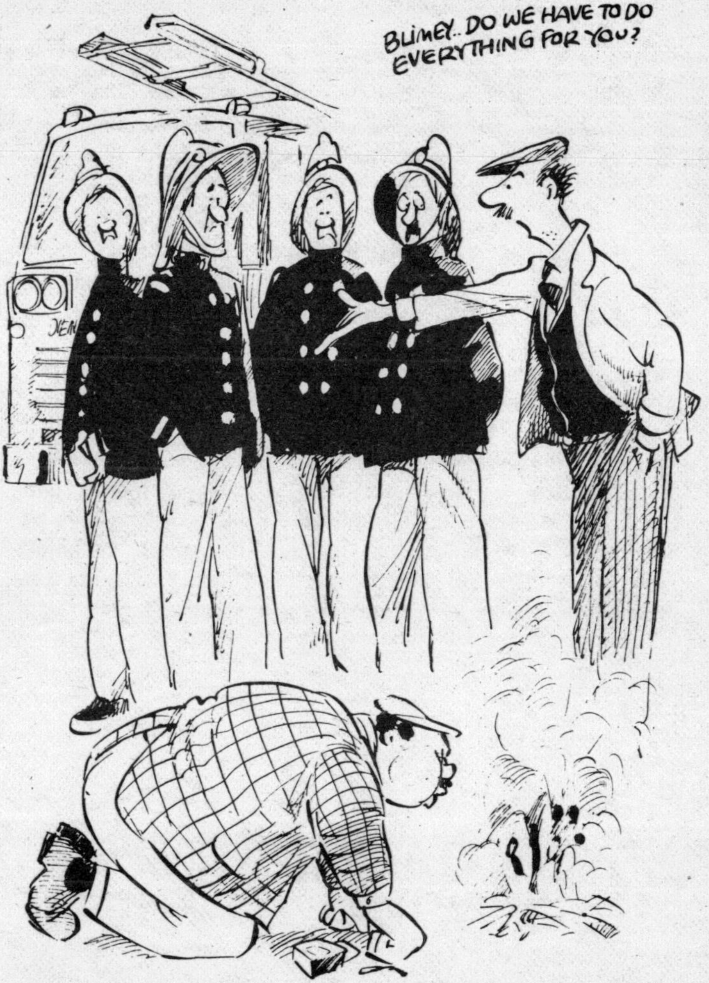
BLIMEY.. DO WE HAVE TO DO EVERYTHING FOR YOU?

DOUBLE-HEADER

It was understandable that prolific portrait-painter Sir Joshua Reynolds would make one cock-up in the course of thousands of canvases. He once painted a man wearing one hat on his head while posing with another under his arm.

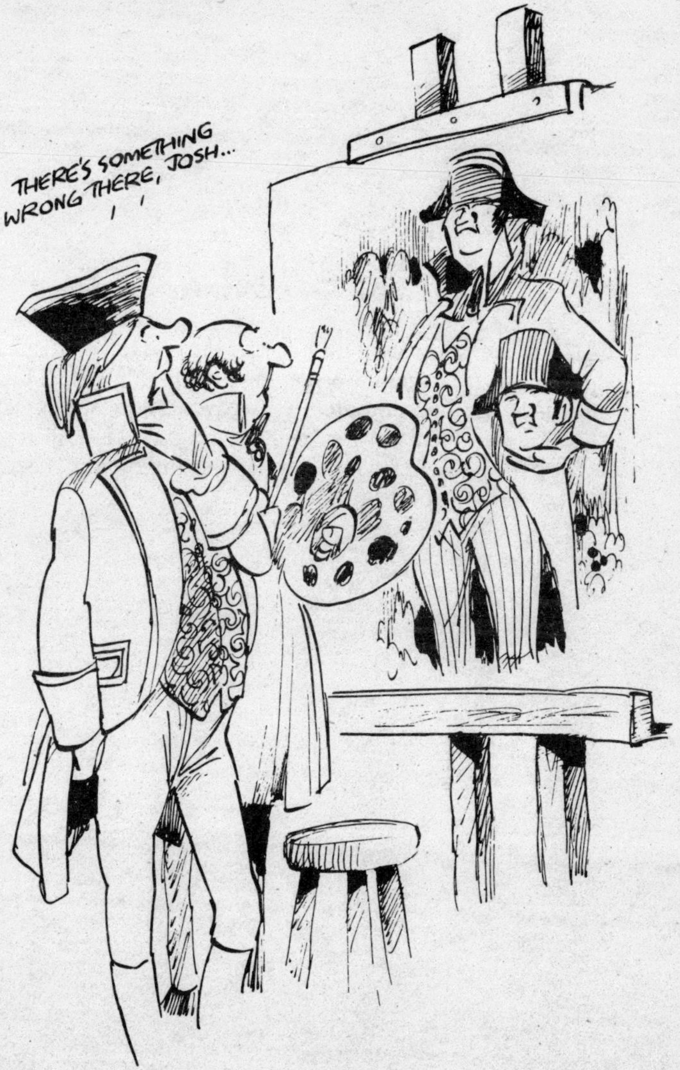
THERE'S SOMETHING
WRONG THERE, JOSH...

HEARTBREAKING

Texas rancher Edward Hill booked into a Dallas hospital for rest and treatment for a minor heart ailment. Three weeks later he had completely recovered and on his way out called at the office for his medical bill. Mr Hill took one look at the £27,000 total, collapsed and died of a heart attack brought on by shock.

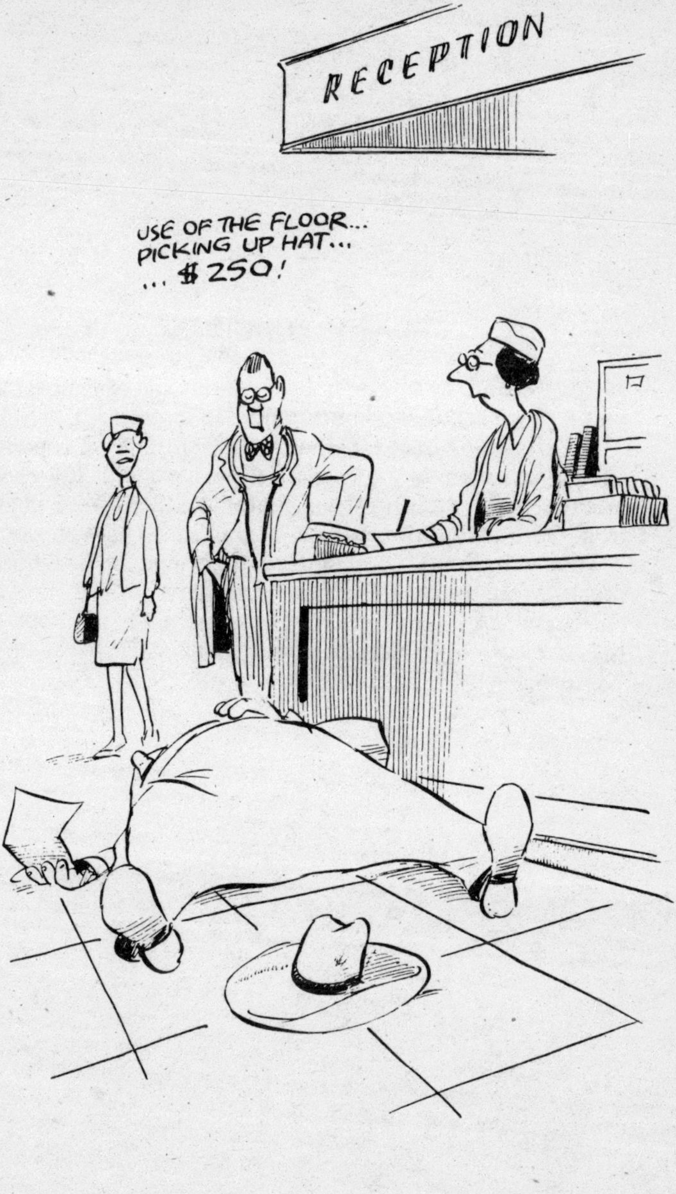
RECEPTION
USE OF THE FLOOR...
PICKING UP HAT...
... $250!

SMILING THROUGH

There were many attempts to invent a pair of false teeth that really worked, and most ended in disaster.

A Parisian dentist, Fouchard, tried to join the top and bottom sets with steel springs. But no one could close their mouths while wearing them. Later dentures were made from teeth taken from corpses at the Battle of Waterloo.

Then later in the nineteenth century came the first world break-through – cheap celluloid choppers. Sadly there was one drawback – they were highly inflammable too. One of the first customers set fire to his teeth when he lit up a cigarette.

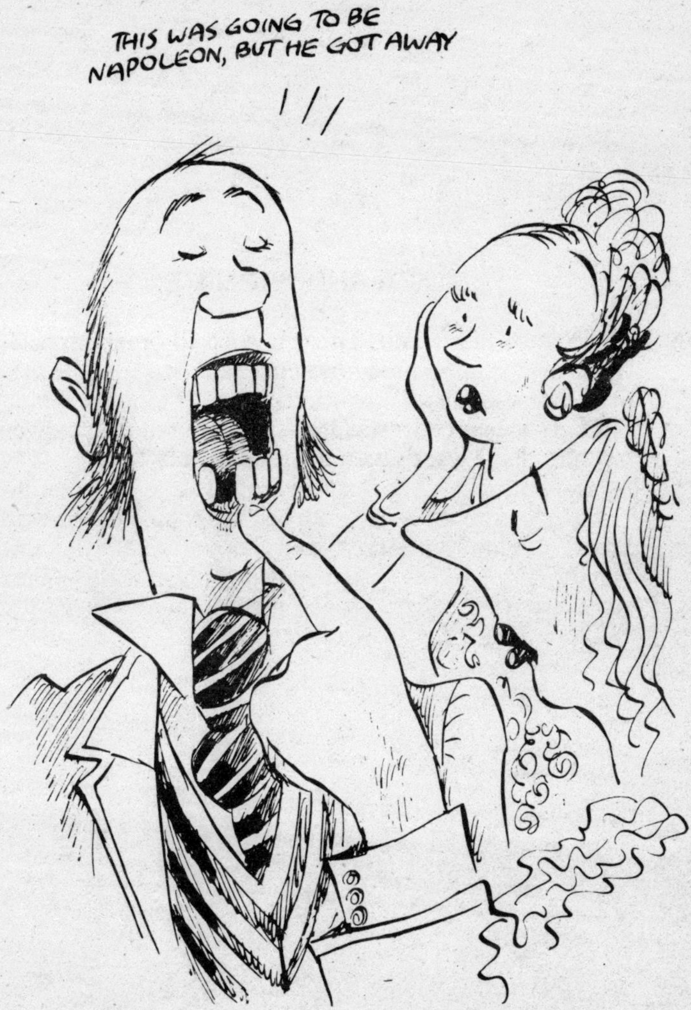
THIS WAS GOING TO BE
NAPOLEON, BUT HE GOT AWAY

MOSES AND THE G-MEN

Tintoretto, the famous artist, needed to brush up on his history. He once painted *Israelites Gathering Manna in the Wilderness* in oils.

Everyone agreed it was a fine picture – but didn't anyone tell him that Moses's men didn't have guns?

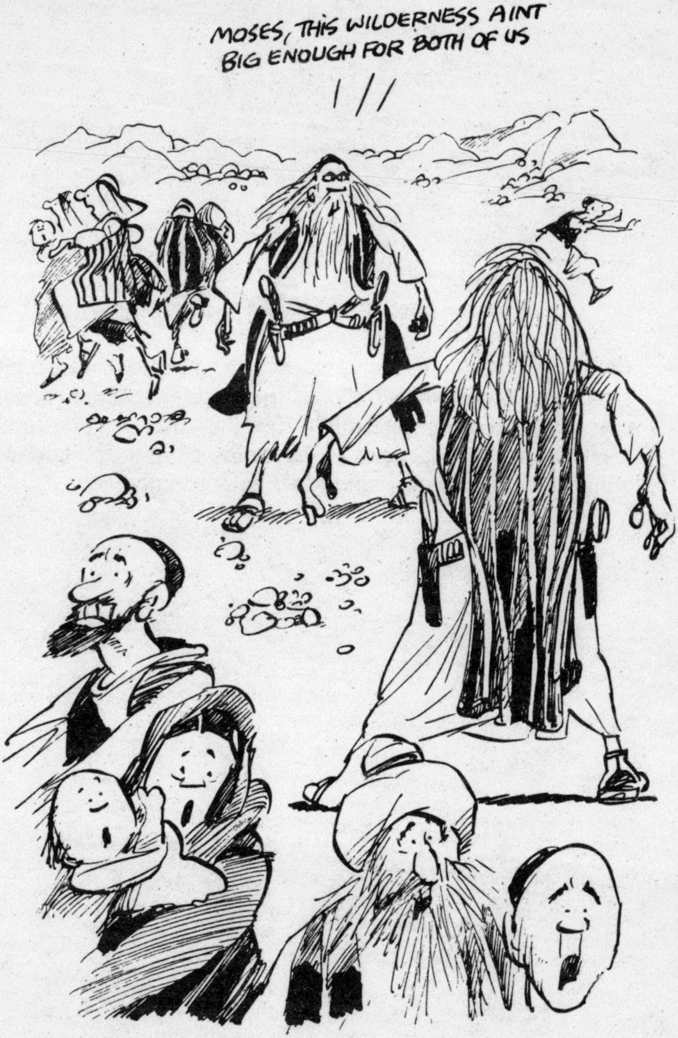
MOSES, THIS WILDERNESS AINT BIG ENOUGH FOR BOTH OF US

PUSH-OFF

Police threatened to give a pram race in Banbury, Oxford-shire, the push when they counted the casualties. In the charity event, twelve people suffered injuries, from broken legs to cuts and bruises. One pram demolished a shop window and another collided with an ambulance.

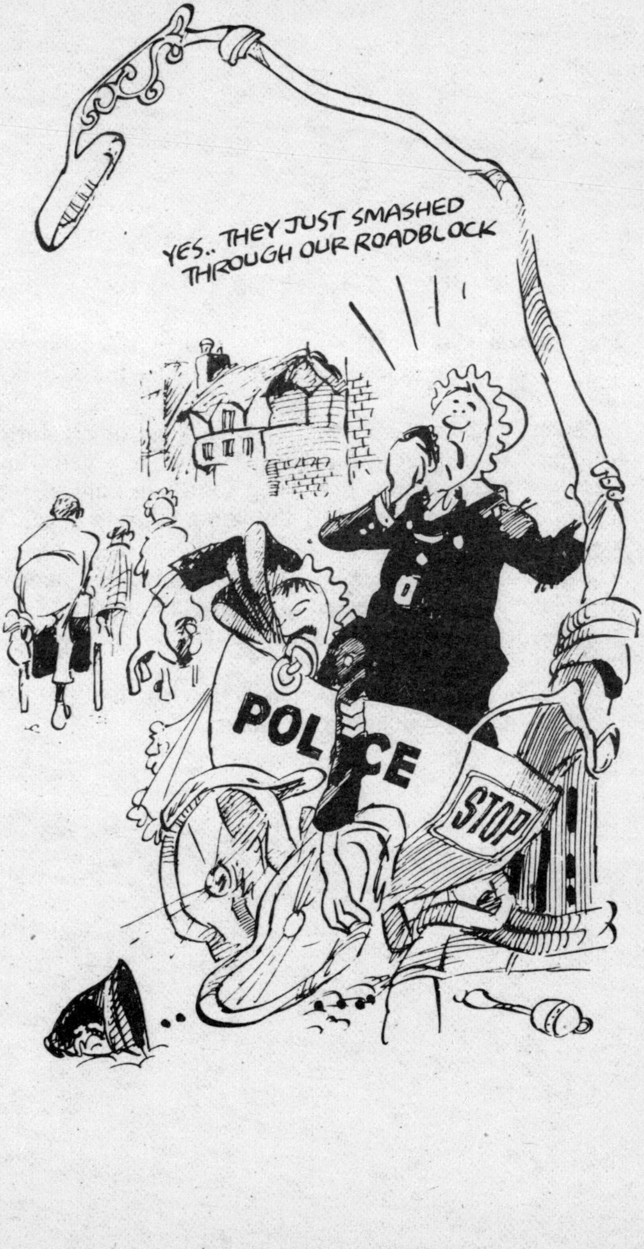
YES.. THEY JUST SMASHED THROUGH OUR ROADBLOCK
POLICE
STOP

A BLOW TO THEIR CHANCES

The Liberal Club, Nantwich, was top of three bowling leagues until strange events began to reduce their chances of staying there.

Players could not believe their eyes when bowls started rolling in all directions on the £10,000 prize green which was only three months old. Then foot-high lumps began to appear and, worse still, the ground itself began to wobble and shake.

The problem was caused by a firm tunnelling beneath their feet using compressed air to dig a new sewer. The green was turned into a giant moving carpet with air ballooning underneath it.

The Liberal Club had opened its new green after losing the previous one under a road scheme.

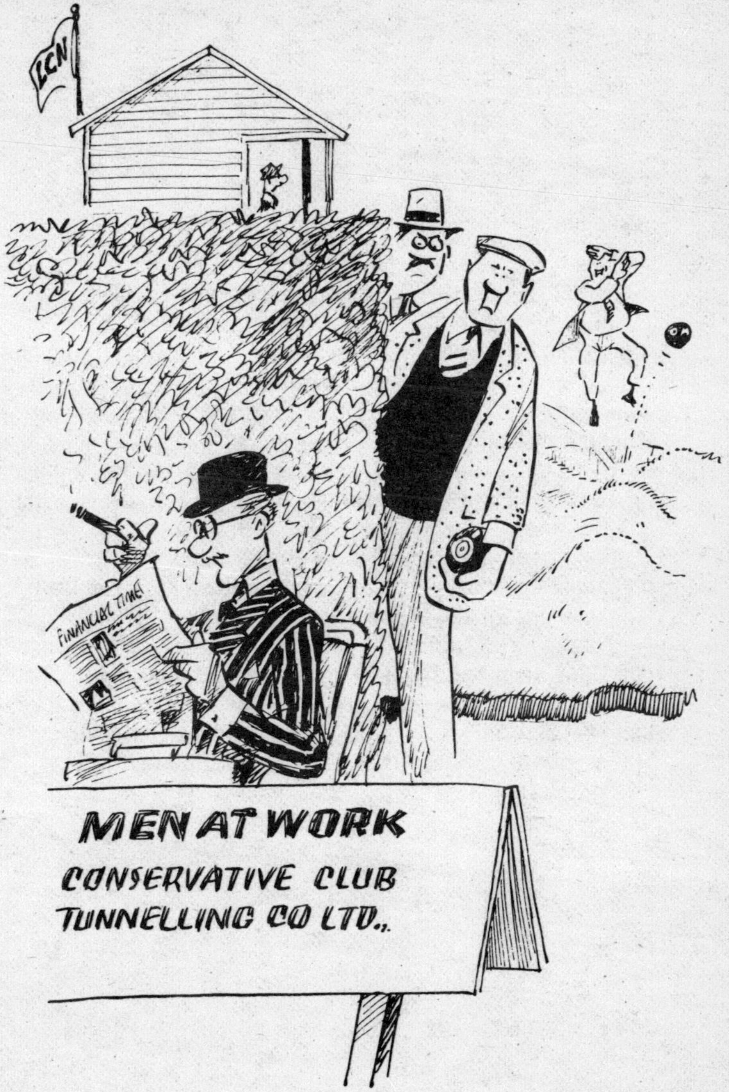
LCN
FINANCIAL TIMES
MEN AT WORK
CONSERVATIVE CLUB
TUNNELLING CO LTD.,

THE WORST APOCALYPTIC EXCUSE

In 1925 Californian Margaret Rowan announced that the world would end on February 13th. She knew it was true because the Archangel Gabriel had given her a full list of the arrangements.

In true Californian style there was an instant wave of suicides and injuries attributed to people trying to climb mountains.

Newspapers in New York were flooded with advertisements from housepainter Robert Reidt asking a multitude to join him for the Apocalypse.

As the clocks chimed out the fateful hour crowds threw up their arms wailing, 'Gabriel, Gabriel, Gabriel!'

But the minutes ticked by and they were all still there – and no Gabriel. A miffed Robert Reidt told the battery of press photographers that their flashbulbs had scared off the Archangel.

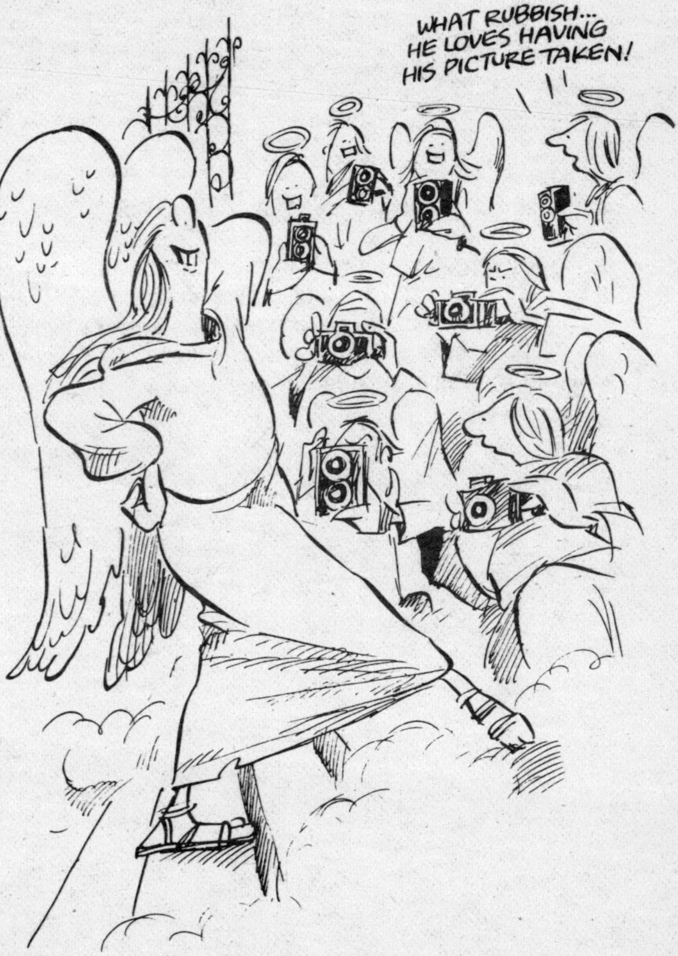
WHAT RUBBISH...
HE LOVES HAVING
HIS PICTURE TAKEN!

ANGIE'S LITTLE ARROWS

Everyone ducked the night Angie Shuttleworth took part in a darts contest in Kenya. The match was officially abandoned when her first dart stuck in a waiter's neck, the second punctured a stuffed antelope head hanging on the wall and the third speared her dog.

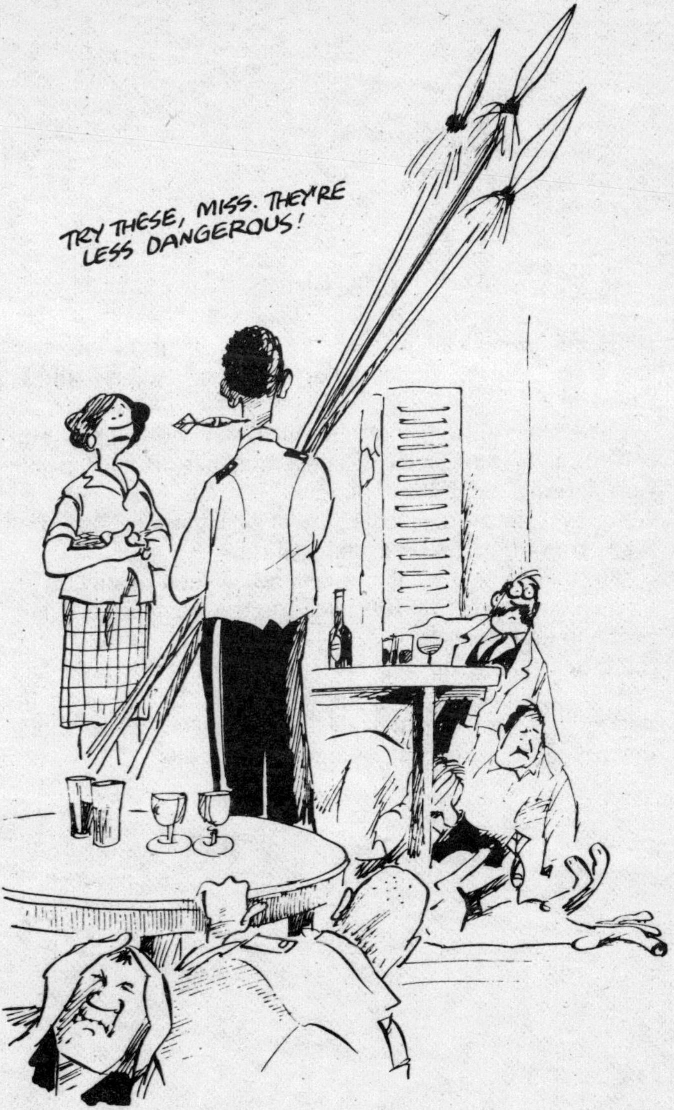
TRY THESE, MISS. THEY'RE LESS DANGEROUS!

MATCHLESS

Luther Hempel had just one burning ambition – to win the West German model-making contest held annually in Cologne.

Each year Luther locked himself away with his glue and collection of thousands of spent matches. But he never won a thing. So Luther planned The Big One. For two years he toiled on a scale model of Cologne Cathedral made from matches painstakingly stuck together.

On the eve of the competition he decided to stay up all night guarding his masterpiece in case rivals or burglars broke in and stole it.

Luther pulled up a comfy armchair, lit his pipe and settled down for a long night's watch. Before long he nodded off, dropped the pipe and started a blaze which destroyed the cathedral and half the house.

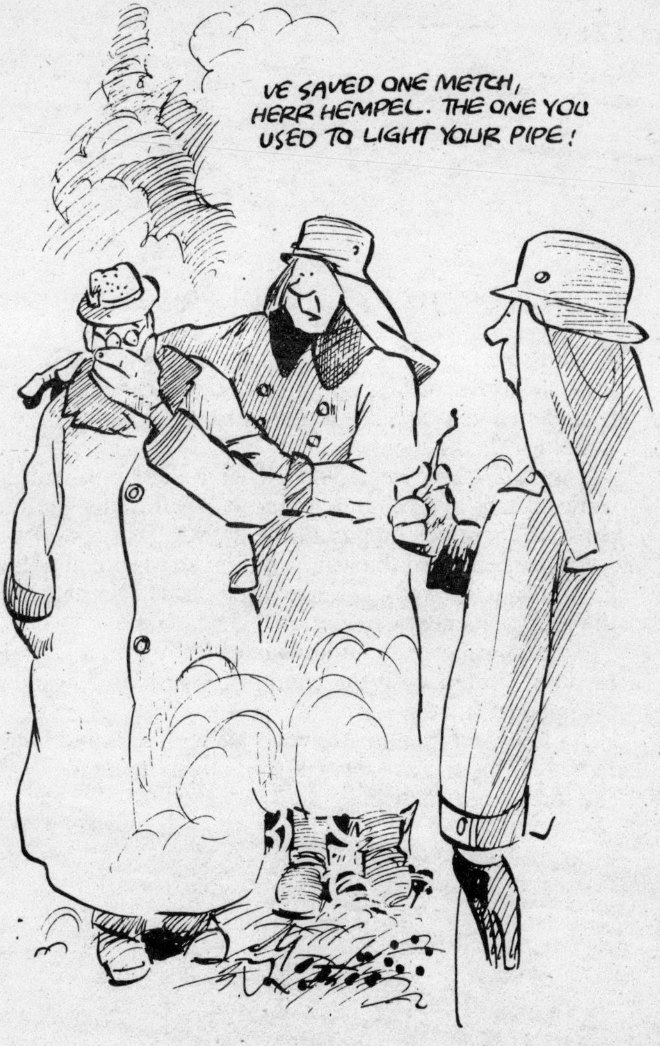
VE SAVED ONE METCH, HERR HEMPEL. THE ONE YOU USED TO LIGHT YOUR PIPE!

THE MOST UNSUCCESSFUL PRISON ESCAPE

The prisoner peeling spuds in the canteen at Northeye Prison, Sussex, always had his eye on a chance to escape. It came when a delivery wagon arrived loaded with vegetables for the kitchen.

The forty-three-year-old convict waited until warders were looking the other way and crawled under the lorry chassis. There he clung until the delivery was complete.

Officers checked the wagon but failed to spot him. Soon he was outside wedged under the vehicle speeding down the A27 to its next destination.

An agonising forty minutes later it drew to a halt. The prisoner waited until the sound of voices died away and dropped to freedom.

As he stood up and stretched his legs he found himself in the compound at Lewes Prison twenty-five miles away, the lorry's next delivery.

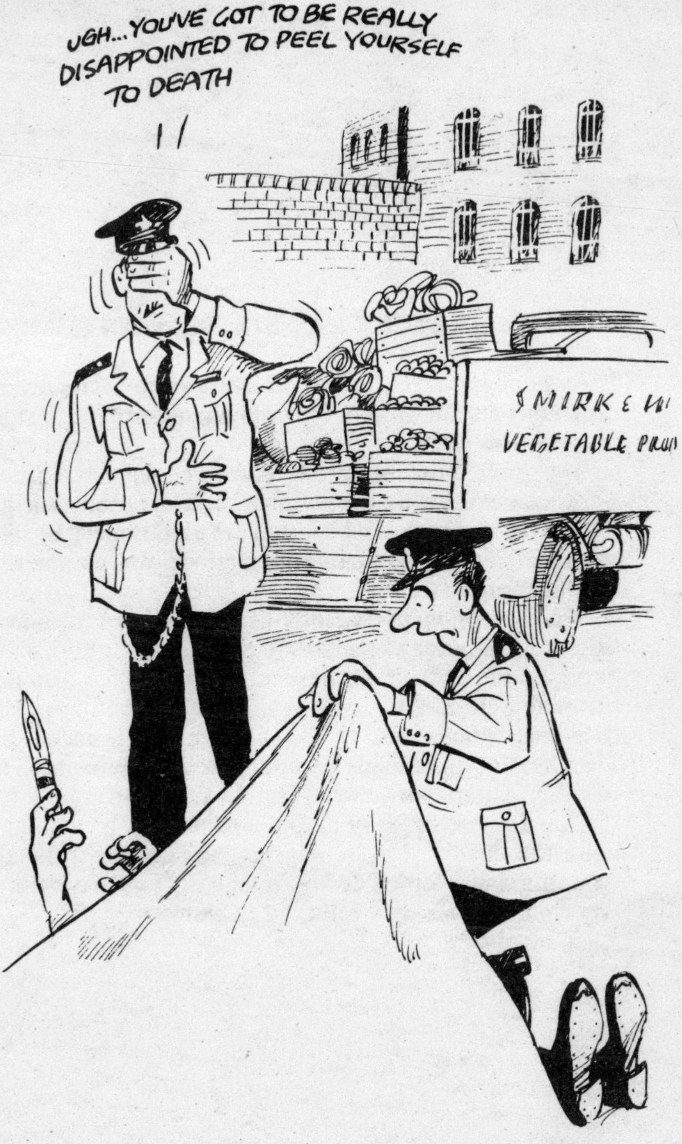
UGH... YOU'VE GOT TO BE REALLY DISAPPOINTED TO PEEL YOURSELF TO DEATH

THE CATCH THAT NO ONE WANTED

Two holidaymakers – Peter Schultz from Germany and Belgian Paul Dewet – were enjoying a fishing trip round the Scottish islands.

They rowed to Gruinard Island which seemed a suitable spot to spend the day, and unpacked their fishing tackle.

Towards evening when they rowed back they were puzzled to see a strange-looking group waiting for them on the mainland.

The reception party, looking like visitors from outer space in helmets and protective garb, grabbed the tourists, stripped off all their clothes and proceeded to scrub them from head to toe.

Police from a nearby NATO base had watched them wander onto the island, forbidden to the public since germ warfare experiments during World War Two.

The pair had landed on Gruinard, heavily contaminated with the deadly disease, anthrax, and despite a forest of warning signs, settled down contentedly for a day's fishing. By amazing luck they returned unharmed.

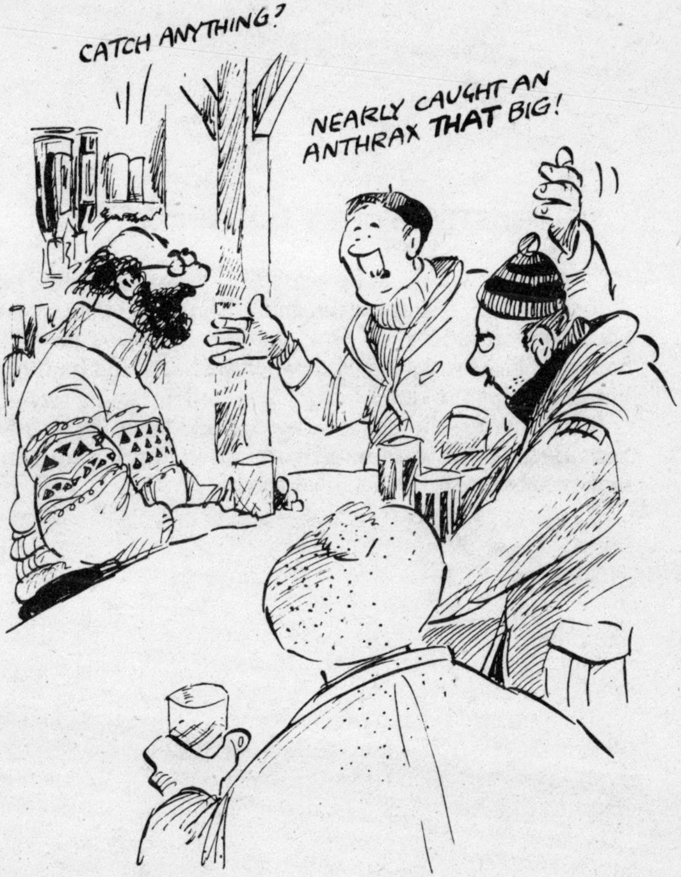
CATCH ANYTHING?
NEARLY CAUGHT AN ANTHRAX THAT BIG!

THE FASTEST POLICE DOG ON TWO LEGS

PC Jim Watts was in hot pursuit of a gang of vandals, but it seemed they might outrun him. 'Stop,' he shouted, 'or I'll set my dog on you.' One of the delinquents instantly halted in his tracks, terrified, when he heard the bark of a berserk alsatian behind him.

But PC Watts did not have a dog – the barks came from him. Back at the station in Bristol his colleagues now call him PC Rover the Official Retriever.

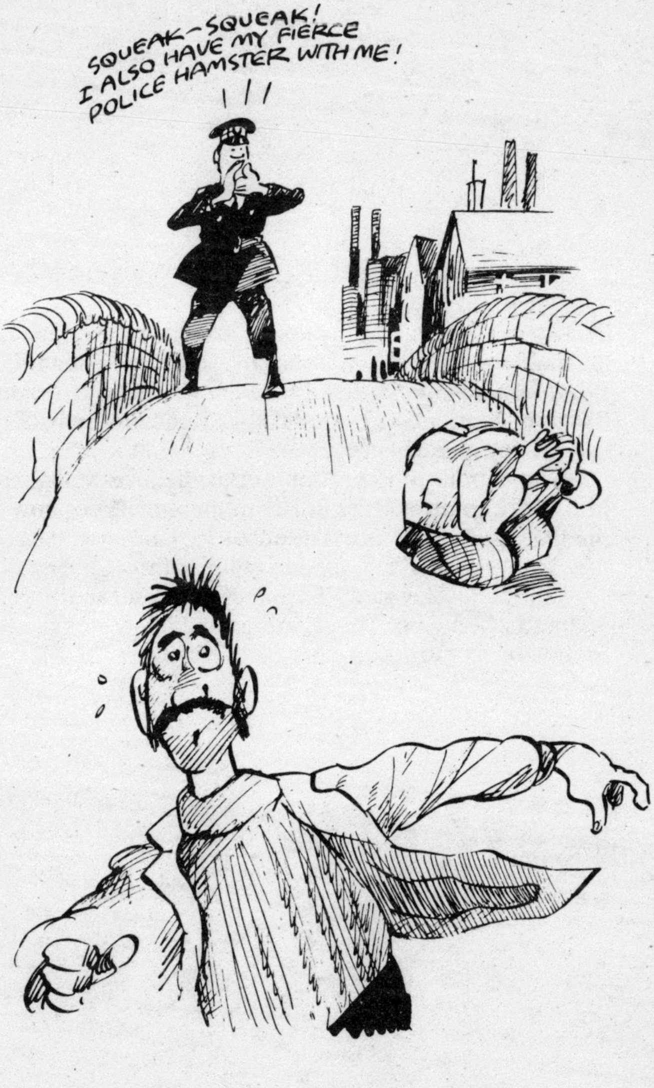
SQUEAK-SQUEAK!
I ALSO HAVE MY FIERCE
POLICE HAMSTER WITH ME!

EVENIN' ALL

A lady in Chorlton, Manchester, had an unexpected visitor as she lay in bed at her terraced home reading a thriller.

An alsatian dog crashed through the ceiling above her. It momentarily hung on its lead while an embarrassed police-dog handler peered down through the hole.

A neighbour at the other end of the terrace had asked the police to investigate noises in the roof. The patrolman had walked along the communal loft-space with his dog until it stepped off a rafter and plunged through the ceiling.

Bob Dunkerley said: 'I looked down and saw a woman sitting in bed with a book in her hand and an expression of horror on her face.'

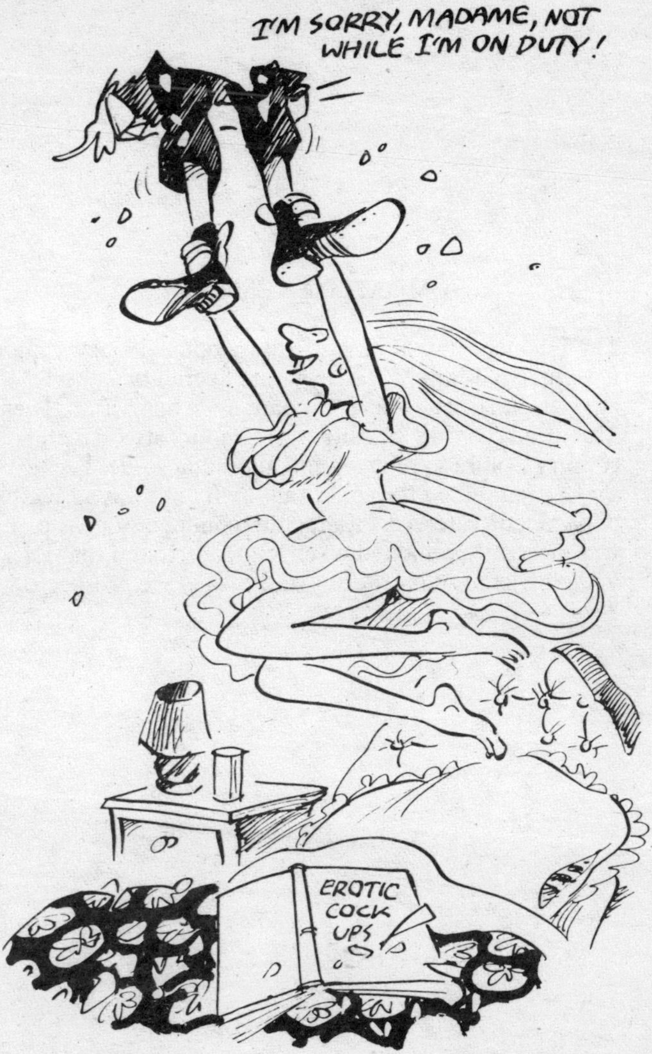
I'M SORRY, MADAME, NOT WHILE I'M ON DUTY!
EROTIC COCK UPS

A MEAL TO REMEMBER

The US Department of Agriculture opened a new canteen for employees in 1977. Agriculture Secretary Robert Bergland decided to officially name it 'The Alfred Packer Memorial Dining Facility' in honour of a nineteenth-century Colorado pioneer and mountain guide. Packer, he said, 'exemplified the spirit and the fare of this agriculture department cafeteria.' Later the commemorative plaque was discreetly removed when someone found that Packer was convicted of murdering and eating five prospectors in 1874.

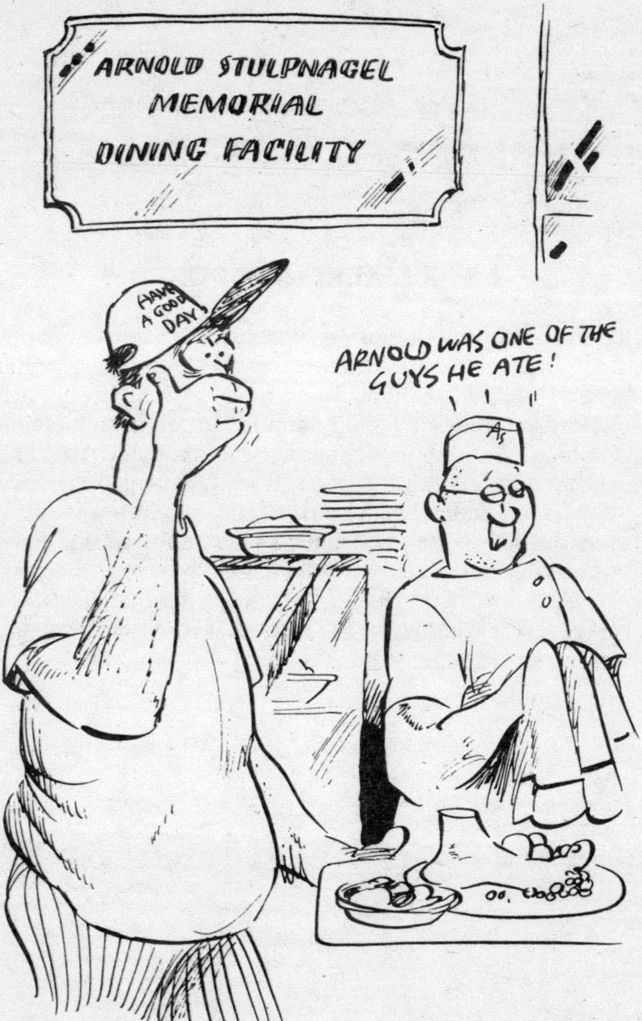
ARNOLD STULPNAGEL
MEMORIAL
DINING FACILITY
HAVE A GOOD DAY
ARNOLD WAS ONE OF THE GUYS HE ATE!
AS

THE KEENEST KEEP-FIT CLUB

Forty statuesque ladies who weighed an average eleven stone each met at Penzance Town Hall for their regular weekly keep-fit session.

It was an energetic affair designed to get the perspiration popping. But the ladies were so enthusiastic that their combined three-ton weight seriously damaged the fabric of the town hall which could cost thousands to repair.

A council spokesman said: 'The whole building literally moved every time they did their exercises.'

The unfortunate ladies, nicknamed the Podgers of Penzance, were banned in the interests of safety and had to search for stronger premises.

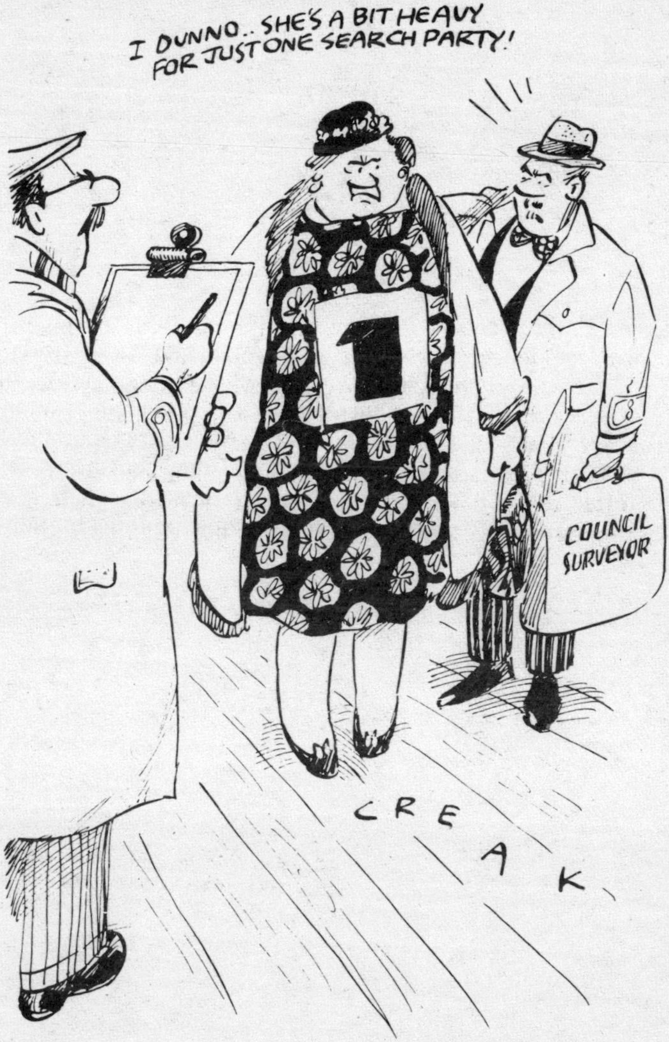
I DUNNO.. SHE'S A BIT HEAVY FOR JUST ONE SEARCH PARTY!
1
COUNCIL SURVEYOR
CREAK

POST EARLY FOR JUSTICE

As Emile Jacquard awaited execution in Paris for murder, new evidence proving his innocence came to light. The judge who had handled the case in Marseilles quickly wrote to the Paris Courts of Justice ordering the death sentence to be quashed.

Poor Jacquard was unfortunately guillotined before the letter reached Paris. Which is not surprising as it took thirty-six years to arrive after being posted in 1902.

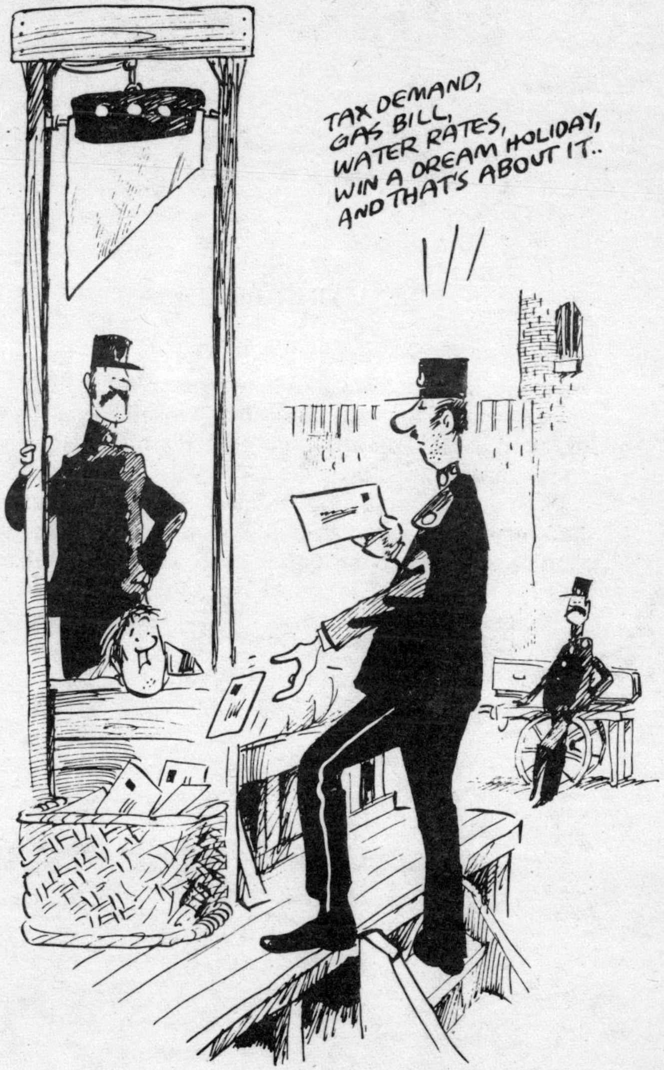
TAX DEMAND,
GAS BILL,
WATER RATES,
WIN A DREAM HOLIDAY,
AND THAT'S ABOUT IT..

A HEARTLESS TASK

When the great English writer Thomas Hardy died he was buried with all due ceremony in Westminster Abbey. At least most of him was. Hardy's last wish was to have his heart buried in the beautiful West Country village churchyard at Stinsford.

That was the plan. But as Hardy's sister prepared for the solemn rite her cat jumped onto the kitchen table where she had left the casket, snatched the great man's heart out of it and disappeared into the garden.

Despite a frantic search of the shrubbery it was never recovered. And unknown to onlookers an empty casket was reverently buried in the graveyard.

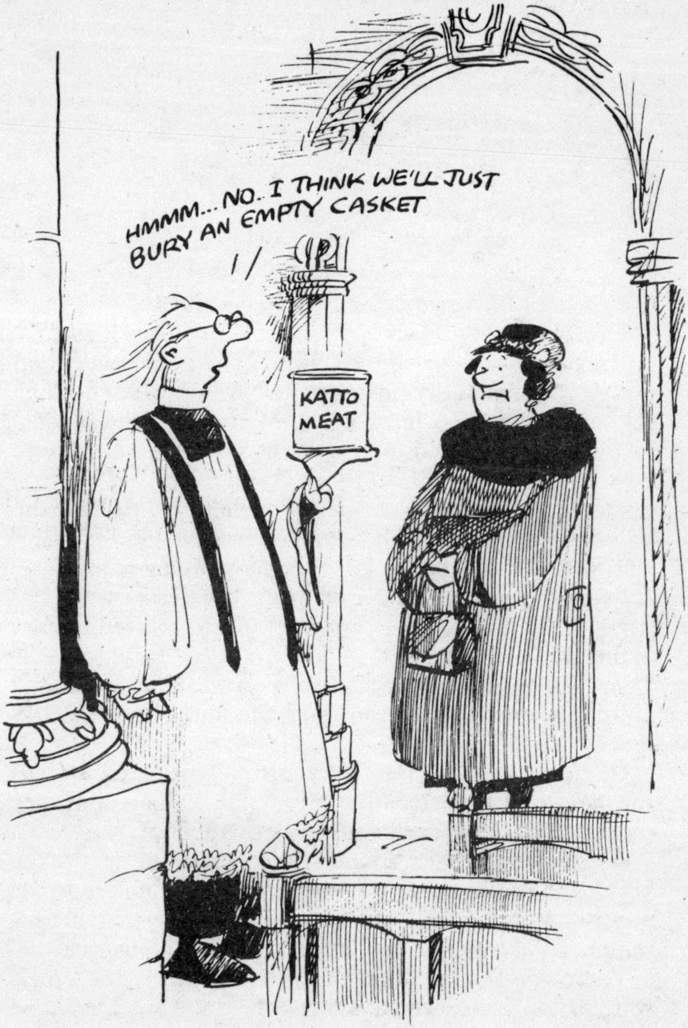
HMMM... NO.. I THINK WE'LL JUST BURY AN EMPTY CASKET
KATTO MEAT

THE WINNER — BY A SHORT HEAD

In February 1885 murderer John Lee walked up the steps of Exeter Prison's newly built scaffold to meet his Maker.

The noose was placed round his neck, the chaplain read the last rites and the hangman pulled the lever. But nothing happened. Lee was led back to his cell while engineers and joiners examined the trapdoor, tested it – and found it working perfectly.

Nineteen-year-old Lee was brought back to face the noose a second time. The chaplain prayed and the hangman pulled the trapdoor lever. Again nothing happened.

By this time Lee must have been wondering what was going on as his presence appeared to be required neither in this world nor the next.

Experts tested the mechanism a second time and found nothing wrong. Lee, familiar with the routine by now, was sent for again.

On the scaffold the last rites were read with some embarrassment and the execution lever pulled. Incredibly Lee remained standing on the motionless trapdoor.

As this could have gone on indefinitely he was taken back to the cells where his sentence was commuted to life imprisonment. Twenty-two years later, after serving his sentence, he was released and emigrated to America.

There was a theory that the chaplain had stood on a warped floorboard which jammed the trapdoor. Each time the engineers tested it he was not present so everything had worked perfectly.

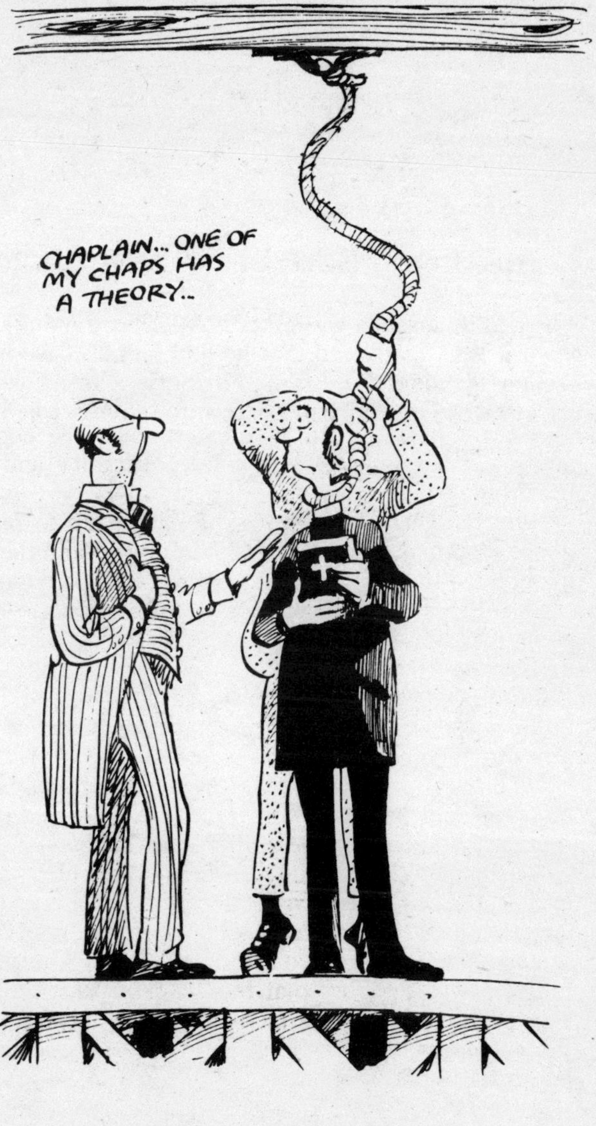
CHAPLAIN... ONE OF MY CHAPS HAS A THEORY..

THE MOST UNSUITABLE CAREER CHOICE

A would-be fireman was asked to quit his training course when it was discovered that he had an obsessive fear of burning buildings. Lancashire Fire Service introduced new tests to weed out other trainees with phobias when some were found to be scared of heights.

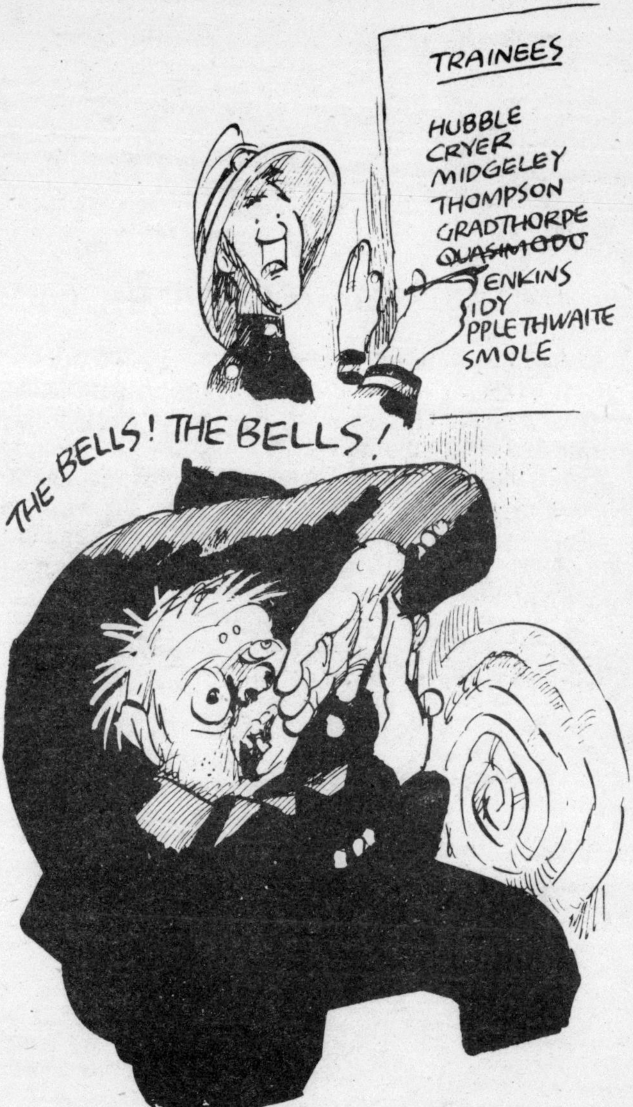
TRAINEES
HUBBLE
CRYER
MIDGELEY
THOMPSON
GRADTHORPE
QUASIMODO
JENKINS
IDY
PPLETHWAITE
SMOLE
THE BELLS! THE BELLS!

DEAD WRONG

Victor Crockett of Swindon thought it was a dead liberty when the Inland Revenue told him his wife Hilda had passed away. They wrote to ask why he was still claiming married man's allowance.

Fifty-seven-year-old Victor said: 'I was very annoyed. I took my wife to the tax office to prove she wasn't dead. But a man there told me she had died on December 8th.

'I said, "You're wrong. She's here with me now." It gave him quite a shock.'

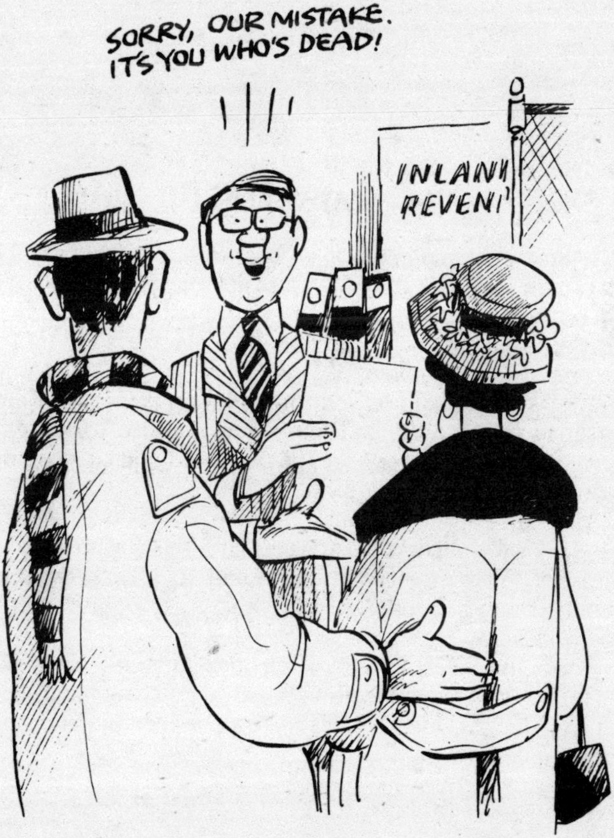
SORRY, OUR MISTAKE.
IT'S YOU WHO'S DEAD!
INLANI
REVENI

THINGS THAT GO BUMP IN THE STREET

A hearse drove solemnly past bustling Broadway Market in London's East End. As it turned an uphill corner the back door swung open and the coffin slid out, crashing into the road where to the horror of shoppers the lid fell off, revealing the corpse.

They shouted and waved to the undertakers who drove on unaware of what had happened. Unsure what to do next, passers-by gingerly replaced the lid and dragged the coffin to the side of the road.

Several pedestrians chuckled nervously at the sight but gave it a wide berth. Five minutes later there was a screech of tyres. The driver had happened to glance over his shoulder and noticed that something wasn't quite right in the back.

The hearse executed a high-speed U-turn and raced back to the market where with as much dignity as they could muster the pair loaded the missing box into the back and glided solemnly on their way.

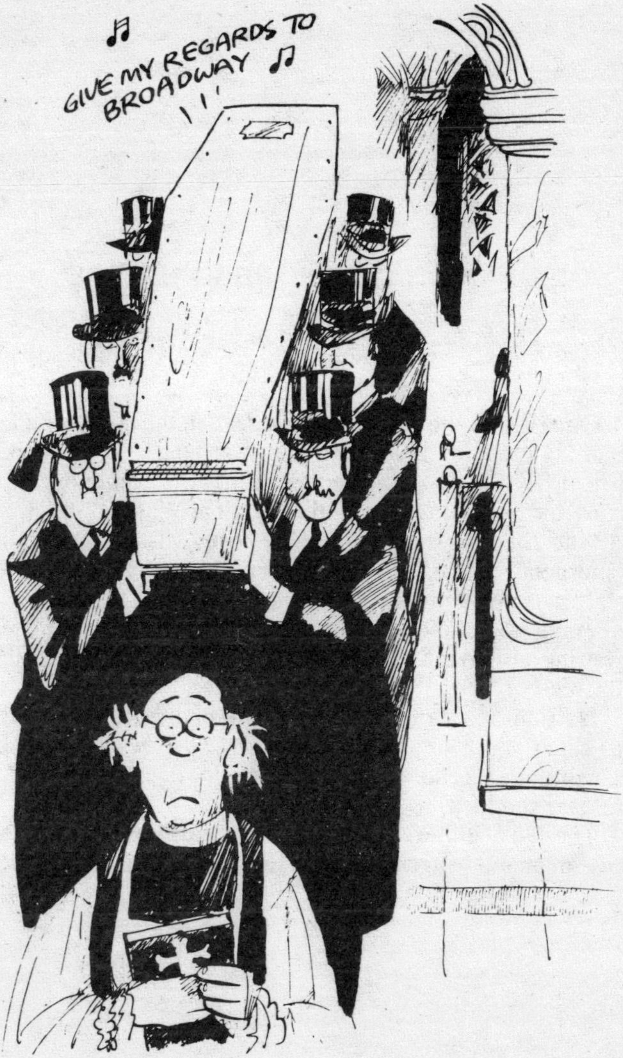
GIVE MY REGARDS TO BROADWAY

OH DEAR WHAT CAN THE MATTER BE . . .

As the 14.15 Manchester–Euston express rattled through the countryside a little old lady left her seat to visit the loo.

Once inside she became trapped when the door jammed. She shouted for help until she was hoarse, but no one heard her. In desperation she pulled the communication cord and the train screeched to a halt at Watford Junction.

And there it stayed – unable to move again until the emergency brake lever inside the toilet was re-set. Railway staff wrestled with the door lock as trains to London began queuing up behind the stranded express. Even passengers waiting to leave Euston were delayed as all efforts failed to free her.

Half-an-hour later, as the rail system threatened to grind to a halt, a porter arrived with a screwdriver and removed a ventilation grille in the lavatory door, enabling him to release the lock.

The lady, in her sixties, emerged blushing with embarrassment and begged rail officials not to reveal her identity.

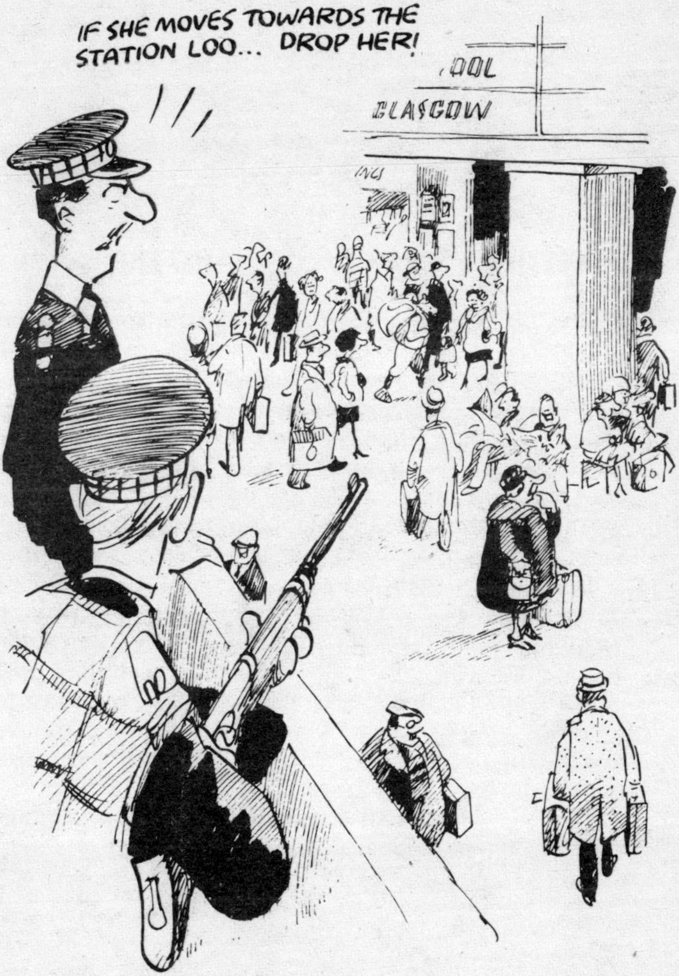
IF SHE MOVES TOWARDS THE STATION LOO... DROP HER!
GLASGOW

THE MOST UNSUCCESSFUL HIGH-RISE SUICIDE

New York can be a lonely place at Christmas. In 1977 down-and-out artist John Helms could not face the future. His life was a mess so he took a lift to the top of the Empire State Building and decided to jump off and end it all. Luckily he made a mess of that too.

As he launched himself from the 86th floor a gust of wind blew him onto a ledge one floor below. Helms interpreted this as Divine intervention and knocked on an office window to ask if he could come in.

It was a television station, and a man who looked up from his work and saw the figure beckoning to him a thousand feet above Fifth Avenue said: 'I couldn't believe it. You don't see a lot a guys coming through the window of the 85th floor.'

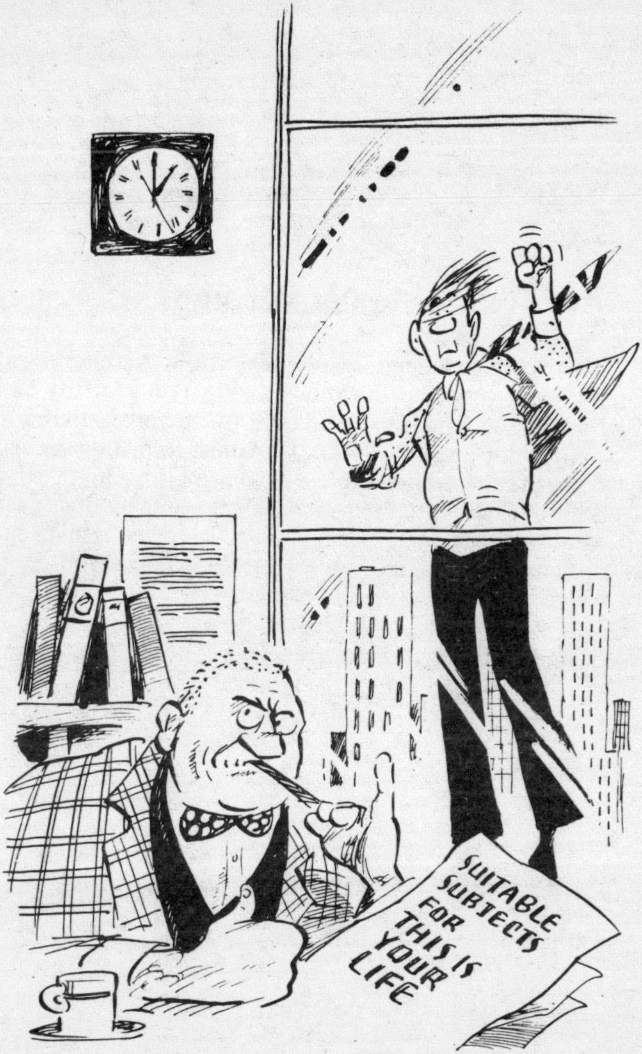
SUITABLE
SUBJECTS
FOR
THIS IS
YOUR
LIFE

SHELLSHOCKED

According to legend, Greek playwright Aeschylus, noted for a shiny bald head, sat down to rest on a Sicilian beach. Nearby, an eagle swooped on a turtle and carried it aloft to look for a suitable stone on which to drop it and crack open the shell. He picked Aeschylus, killing him instantly.

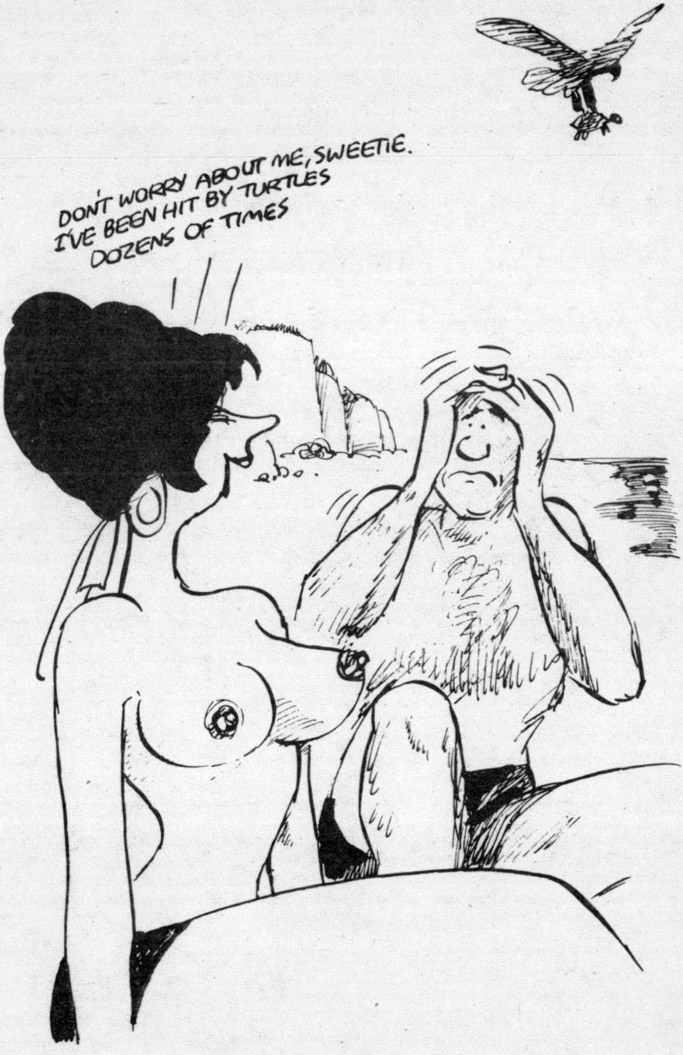
DON'T WORRY ABOUT ME, SWEETIE.
I'VE BEEN HIT BY TURTLES
DOZENS OF TIMES

THE MOST EASILY EXECUTED SKYJACK

In 1976 an armed hi-jacker boarded a plane in New York and as soon as it was airborne pulled out his gun and jabbed it at the nearest stewardess, who later reported the following conversation:

Hi-jacker: 'This plane is gonna fly to Detroit.'

Stewardess: 'That's right, sir. This is the scheduled flight to Detroit.'

Hi-jacker: 'Oh good. Very good.'

And he sat down again and put the pistol back in his pocket.

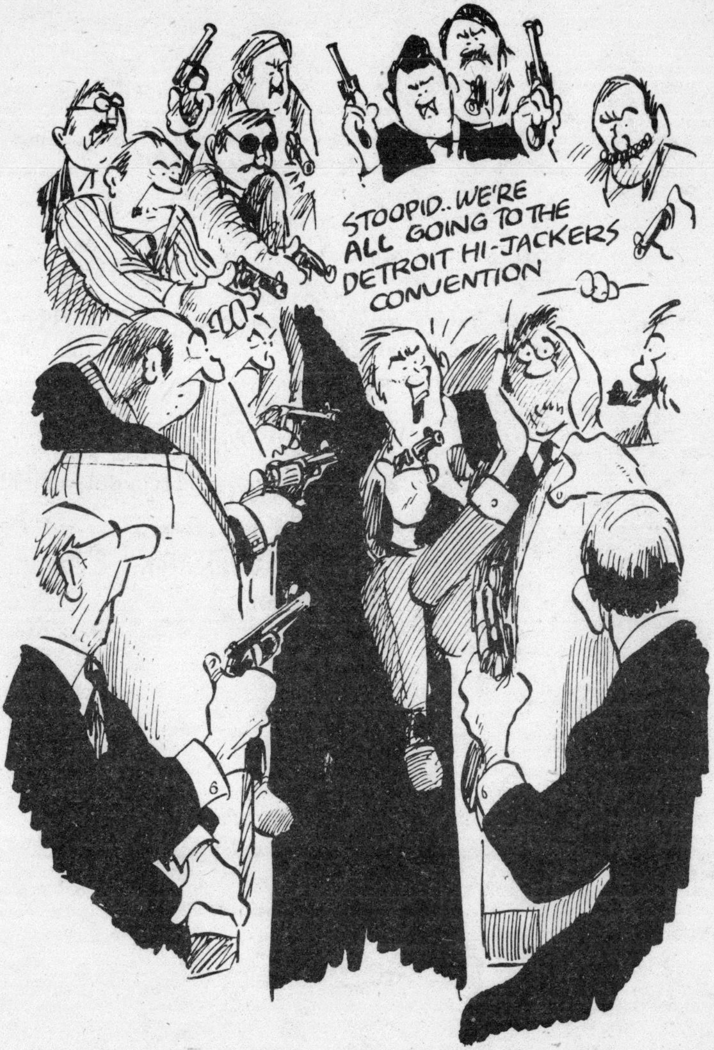
STOOPID.. WE'RE ALL GOING TO THE DETROIT HI-JACKERS CONVENTION

GREAT WEDDINGS OF OUR TIME

Guests at the Chelsea wedding glanced anxiously at their watches as they awaited the arrival of the bride. Eight minutes after the appointed hour there was still no sign of her, and the bridegroom passed out with the tension. The best man took one look at him stretched out on the floor and he fainted too.

At this moment the bride arrived escorted by two brides-maids and all three promptly burst into tears. Then as the bridegroom came to, his wife-to-be surveyed the whole scene and passed out herself.

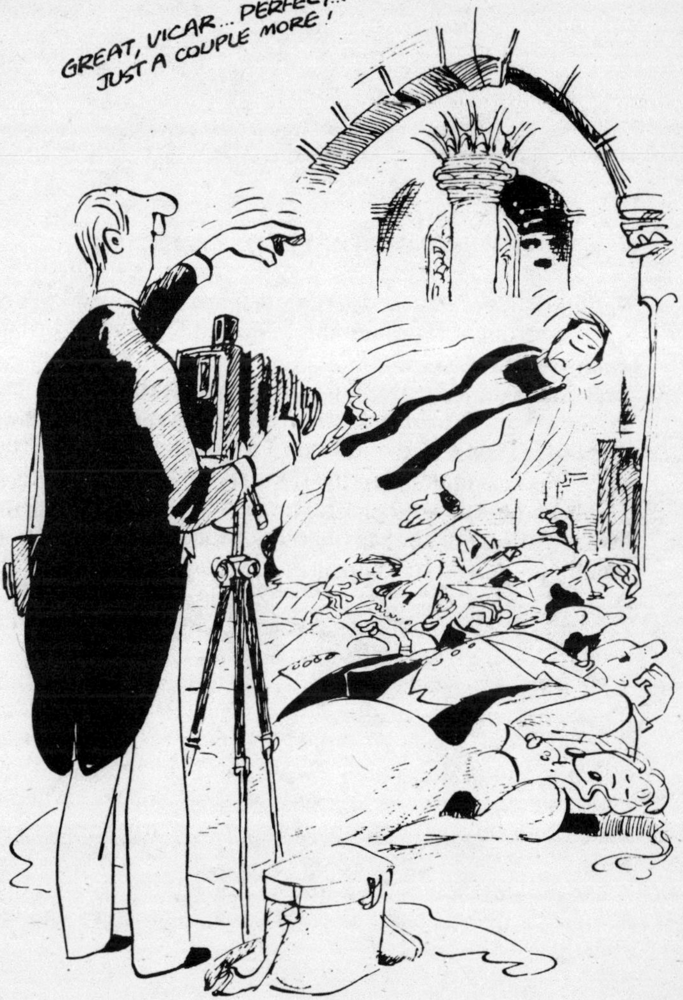
GREAT, VICAR... PERFECT...
JUST A COUPLE MORE!

GREAT BRITISH HOLIDAYS – 1

Walter Philips, who had been off work for several years suffering from nervous debility, decided to take a relaxing holiday by the sea.

As his train sped through Devon, fifty-six-year-old Mr Philips decided to check that the carriage door worked properly. 'I tend to panic when I'm getting off trains,' he said. 'I like to make sure the door is easy to open.'

Before he knew what was happening the express slipstream tore open the carriage door taking anxiety-prone Mr Philips with it. He clung on horizontally by his fingertips as the train thundered towards Newton Abbot.

'It was a lonely feeling,' he said later. 'I could feel the strength draining out of my arms as we sped along.'

He let go but managed to grab the next window through which sixty-nine-year-old grandfather Bill Gentry was gazing. 'I saw a pair of hands and a face. The man was shouting "Stop the train." He was a tall chap and I don't know where I got the strength to drag him in. When I pulled him through he fainted and I went off for a cup of tea.'

Mr Philips stayed one night at his holiday hotel in Torquay and returned home. 'I decided I had seen enough of Devon,' he said.

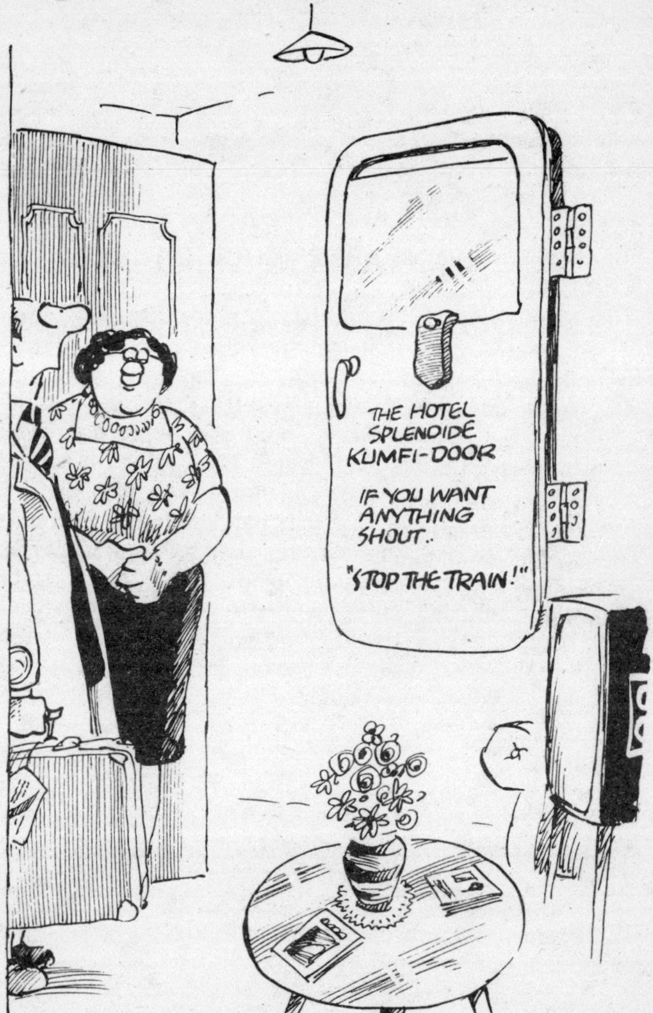
THE HOTEL SPLENDIDE KUMFI-DOOR
IF YOU WANT ANYTHING SHOUT..
"STOP THE TRAIN!"

SOMETHING TO CHEW OVER

Bungling German bank robber Hans Schaarschmidt was arrested as he carried out a raid near Leipzig in 1907.

He was incarcerated for six years in a medieval jail with a solid oak cell door and iron-hard wooden bars. Very soon Schaarschmidt evolved an escape plan. He decided to gnaw his way out.

Every night after lights-out he set to work chewing the bars. Seven months later he had eaten them away and was out. He immediately went back to the bank near Leipzig to finish off the robbery and was arrested again within minutes.

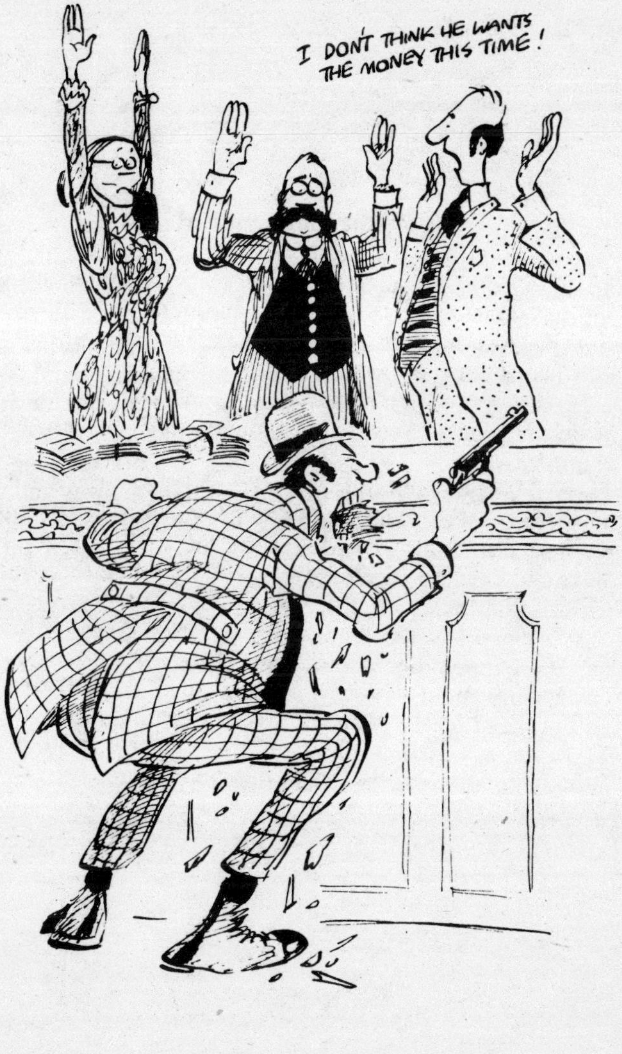
I DON'T THINK HE WANTS THE MONEY THIS TIME!

IT'S A DOG'S LIFE

In the 1950s US postmen, tired of being bitten by the nation's dogs, appealed to the government for help. Three main suggestions emerged from the official committee that sat to consider the problem.

1: All US postmen should be sprayed from head to foot in dog repellent. Wives and families were not consulted about this.

2: All US postmen should have their legs wrapped in wire mesh to protect them from canine attack. The postmen pointed out that backsides were the major target and all-round chicken wire protection could prove to be more painful than a dog bite.

3: Official wisdom finally excelled itself with a solution based on animal behavioural psychology. All US postmen when confronted with a dog were to whip off their hats and proceed up the path with them stuck over their faces. The theory was that this would sufficiently confuse the animals to allow the postmen time to escape.

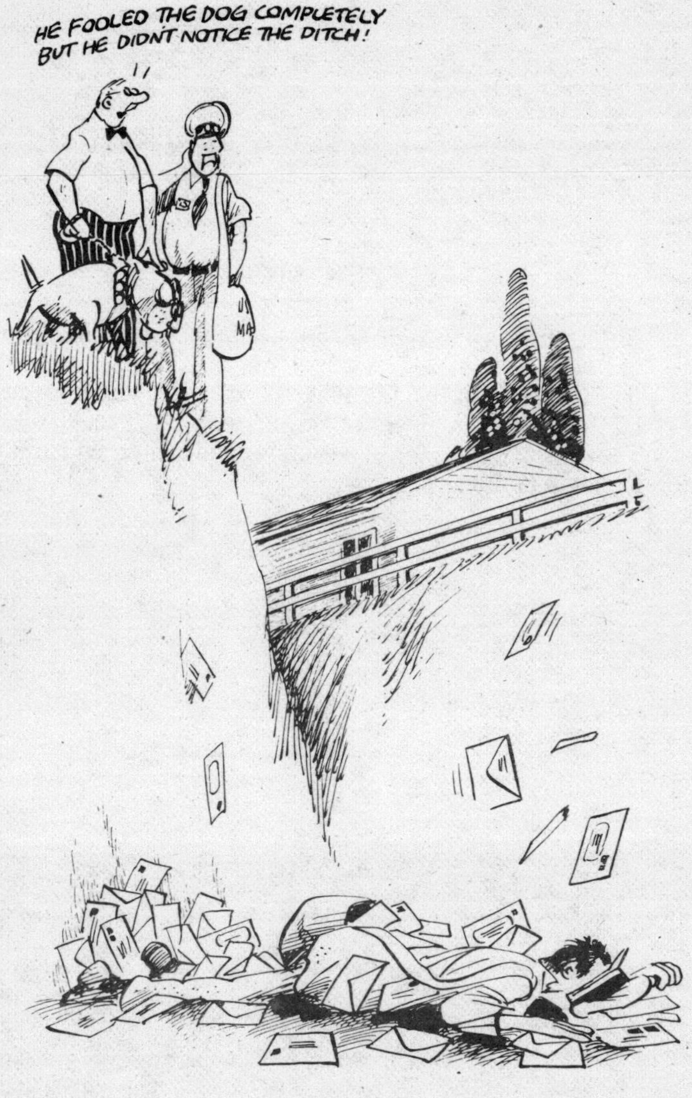
HE FOOLED THE DOG COMPLETELY
BUT HE DIDN'T NOTICE THE DITCH!

TAKING STOCK

Boston town council decided it needed to invest in a pair of stocks back in 1634. A carpenter named Palmer seemed the right man for the job. When the contract was complete he presented the elders of Boston with a bill for £1.13s. They arrested him for overcharging and sentenced him to a stretch in the new stocks.

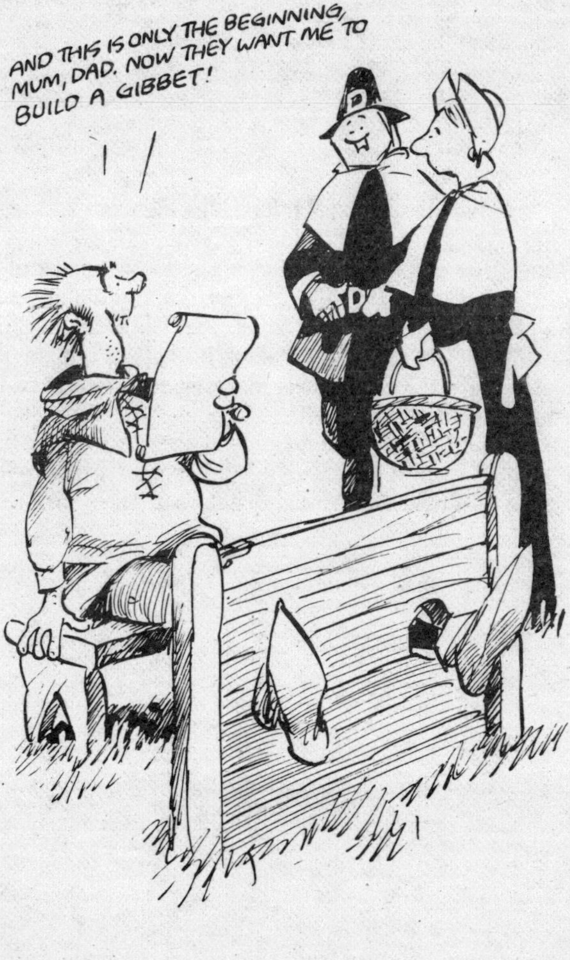
AND THIS IS ONLY THE BEGINNING, MUM, DAD. NOW THEY WANT ME TO BUILD A GIBBET!

THE SINGER WHO FLUFFED HIS LINES

Opera fans sat transfixed during a performance of *Rigo-
letto*, not so much at the efforts of a Canadian baritone,
but at the progress of a pigeon feather that floated slowly
down from the roof. It landed in his mouth and the singer,
in full flight, swallowed it, almost choked, and promptly
collapsed.

The house manager at the concert in Chile hurried
onstage to apologise to the audience, tripped over the
soprano's dress and plunged headfirst into the orchestra
pit.

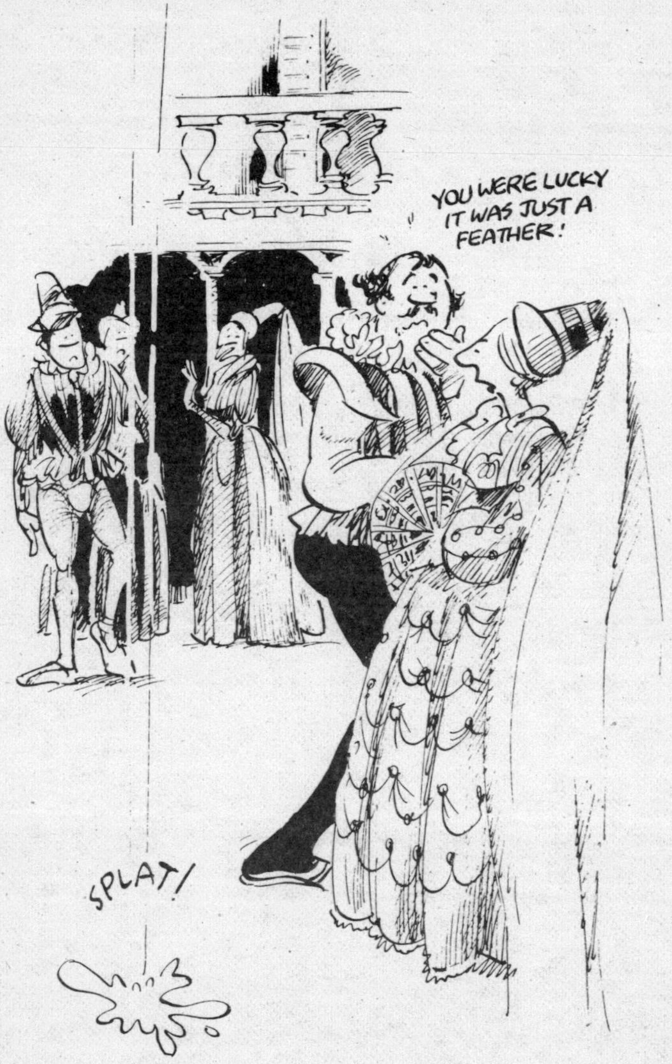
YOU WERE LUCKY IT WAS JUST A FEATHER!
SPLAT!

WATER DIVINER

A Peterborough vicar, the Rev. Philip Randall, had a keen eye for local history. He became fascinated by a stone in his churchyard which had been inscribed with the initials *HWP*. After eight years searching parish records for clues to its identity the cleric discovered that the letters stood for *Hot Water Pipe*.

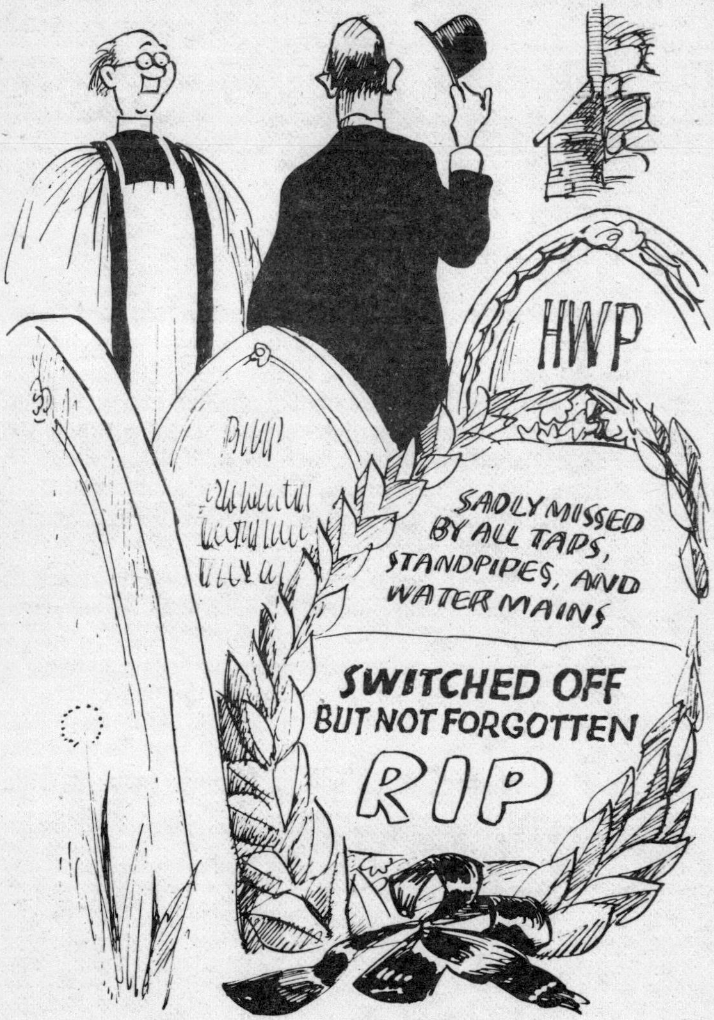
HWP
SADLY MISSED BY ALL TAPS, STANDPIPES, AND WATER MAINS
SWITCHED OFF BUT NOT FORGOTTEN
RIP

GREAT BRITISH HOLIDAYS – 2

Forty-five British tourists booked a coach tour in Austria that turned out to be such a disaster that the survivors have reunions.

Their bus was involved in so many crashes in one 24-hour period that two passengers passed out with the strain. By the time they arrived back in England the six-week-old coach had had its door ripped off and the wing mirror tied on with a passenger's braces. Windows were smashed and all the side panels torn off.

Their trouble began when the coach driver collapsed with a heart attack and an Austrian villager volunteered to drive them home.

The aisle between the seats was stacked so high with twisted metal retrieved from smashes by thoughtful passengers that half a Volkswagen was later found among the scrap.

Back in Blighty, with a baffling impulsiveness only the British can muster, six of them rebooked on the spot for the following year.

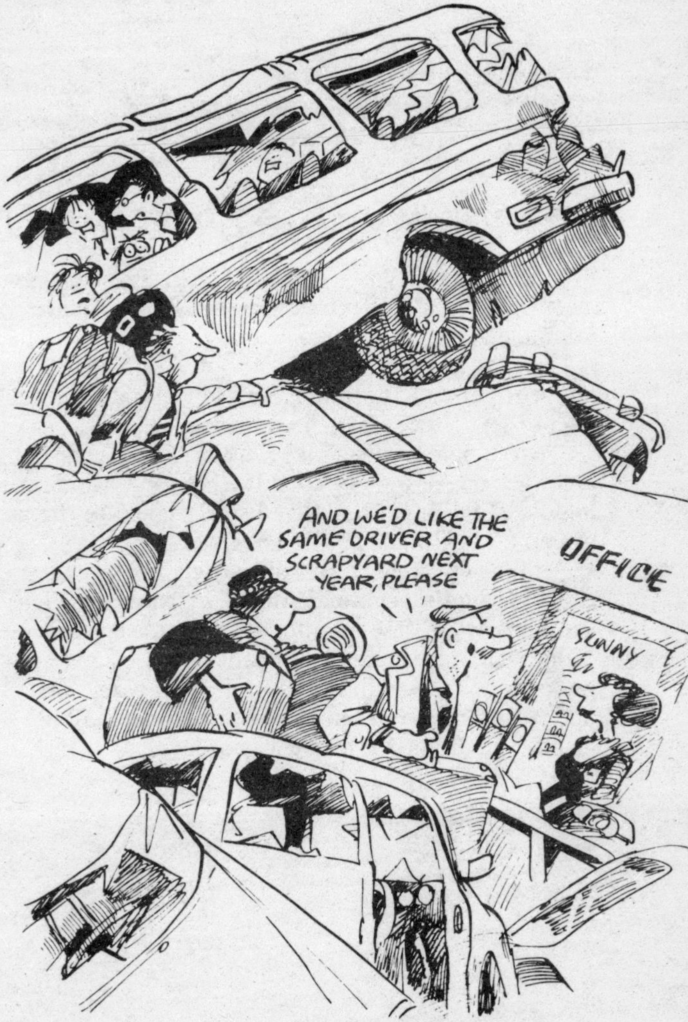
AND WE'D LIKE THE SAME DRIVER AND SCRAPYARD NEXT YEAR, PLEASE
OFFICE
SUNNY

THE DREAM THAT CAME DOWN TO EARTH

Was it a bird? Was it a plane? No, just the figure of sleepwalker Dave Webb disappearing faster than a speeding bullet.

Dave lay in bed at home in Wroot, Doncaster, dreaming about Superman after watching a film about his super hero twenty-seven times on a home video.

Then in a deep sleep Dave, a thirty-four-year-old store boss, got out of bed, opened the bedroom window in the middle of the night and dived stark naked to the ground fifteen feet below.

After he was treated for a dislocated jaw, several cracked ribs and countless cuts and bruises, his wife Pat nailed down the windows in case he attempted a repeat performance.

She said: 'He suddenly jumped out of bed and I saw him go towards the window. Before I could reach him he had opened it and dived out. He is Superman-mad but it is a wonder he didn't kill himself.'

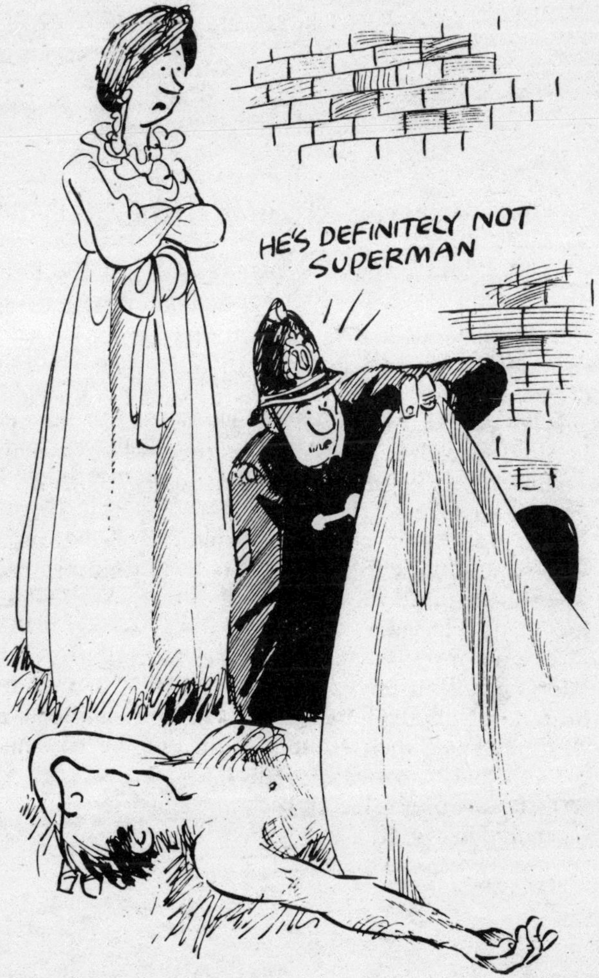
HE'S DEFINITELY NOT SUPERMAN

A BAD CASE OF CLOTH EARS

Late one evening there was a knock at the door of Ann Tomlinson's home in Leeds. It was an emergency doctor who had been called to another Mrs Tomlinson and had the addresses mixed up. Ann pointed out the mistake and directed him on his way.

Next day she received an appointment card from a hospital specialist. Ann delivered the card to the right Mrs Tomlinson and rang the hospital to tell them they had made a mistake.

The next day a hospital consultant called to examine her. Ann politely told him where to put his stethoscope. Then she went to the local health centre to tell them they had made a blunder.

By way of reply Ann opened her front door a few days later to find an ambulance crew waiting to take her to hospital. 'Nobody in this house is ill,' she shouted angrily. But they stood their ground. In the end her sixteen-year-old son had to convince them that everyone was in fine fettle before they reluctantly climbed back into their ambulance and drove off.

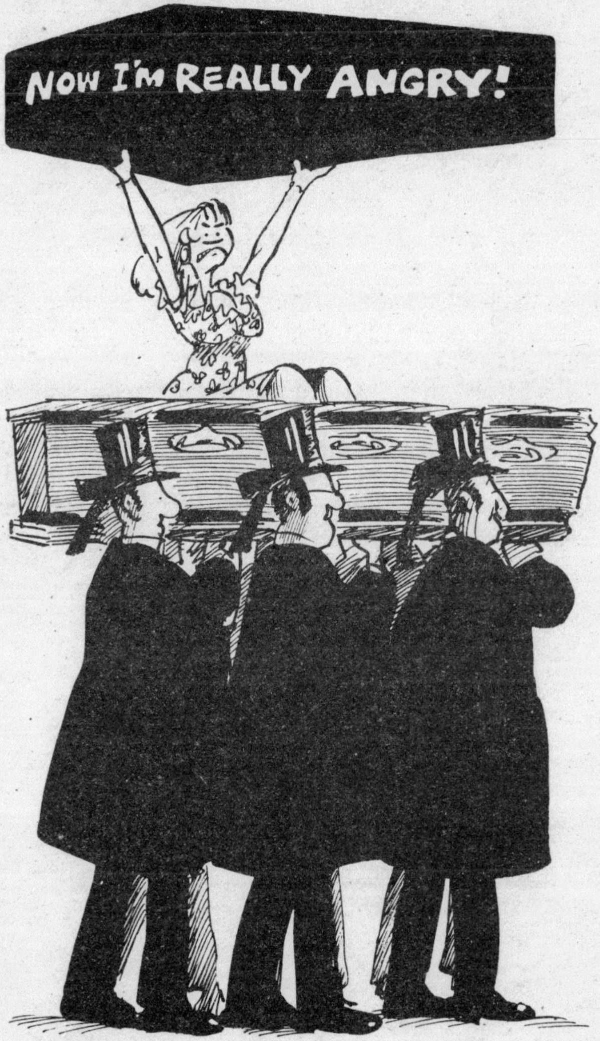
NOW I'M REALLY ANGRY!

LOONY TOONS

The ancient Sybarites loved nothing more than a bit of pomp and pageantry. And to give it all some edge they trained their horses to dance to music.

In 510 BC these early Italians attempted to invade the city of Croton. As the Sybarite cavalry thundered nearer the inhabitants suddenly pulled out musical instruments and struck up a lively tune. The horses immediately broke into a soft-shoe shuffle leaving their riders defenceless against a hail of arrows.

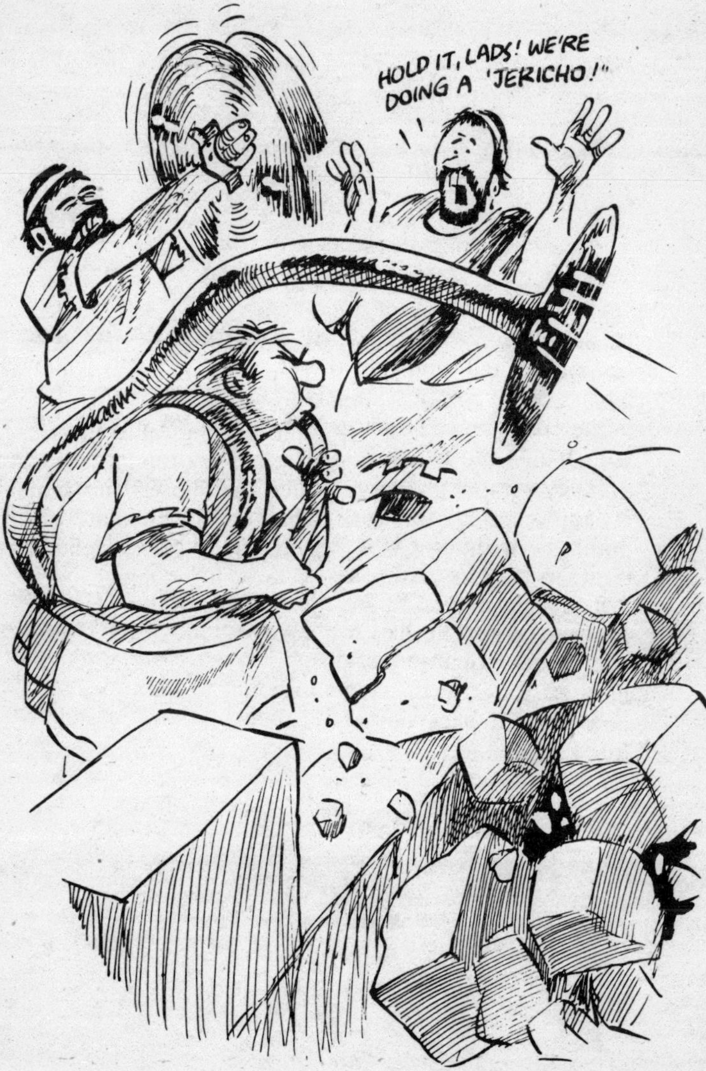
HOLD IT, LADS! WE'RE DOING A 'JERICHO!'

CAUSING A STINK

Ricardo Foreza stood in the dock of a Rio de Janeiro courtroom and admitted the offence. 'It's true,' he confessed. 'I did remove the soap from the men's washroom in the civil service building and swop it for stuff that turns your hands and face black.

'They were so pompous and full of self importance when I had to see them about my tax return. I can't stand pompous people. I had to do something to bring them down to earth.'

The magistrates believed him and let him free with a caution. When he had left an awful smell pervaded the courtroom. Ricardo had dropped a couple of stink bombs because the justices were too pompous. He was arrested and brought back before the bench where his joke cost him a £100 fine.

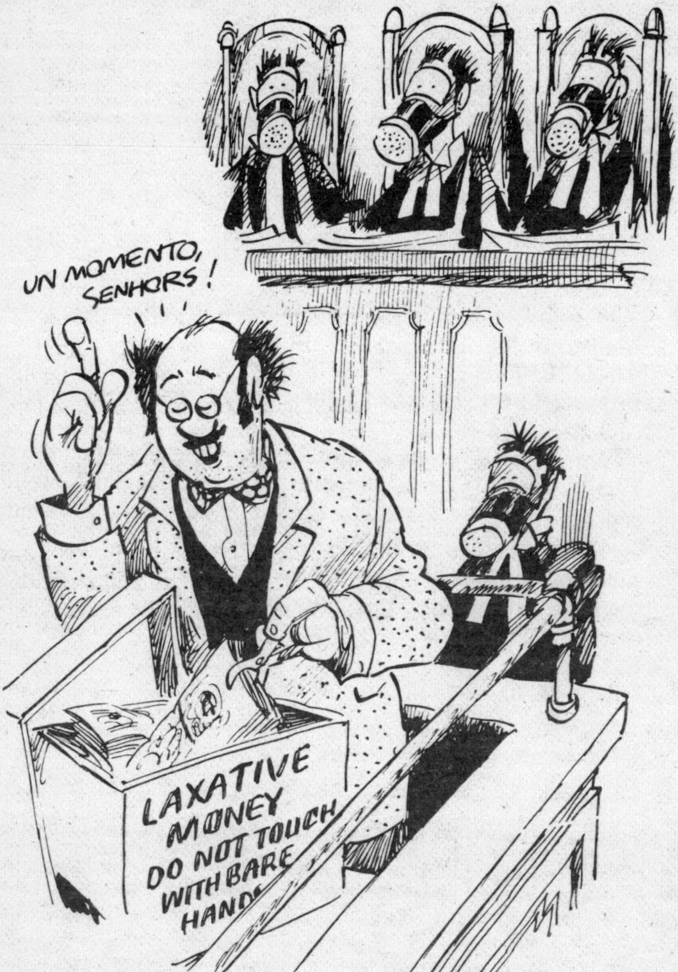
UN MOMENTO, SENHORS!
LAXATIVE MONEY DO NOT TOUCH WITH BARE HAND

THE NEW WAVE

The old London Paragon Theatre prided itself on the realism of its performances. In 1910 the action called for a boat to plough through storm-tossed seas. The effect was produced by a machine which made ripples in a huge tank of water onstage.

When the mechanism broke down, theatre firemen were hastily summoned to create the same effect with hose-pipes.

As they turned up the pressure a connection broke and hundreds of gallons filled the orchestra pit and cascaded over the front row of the audience.

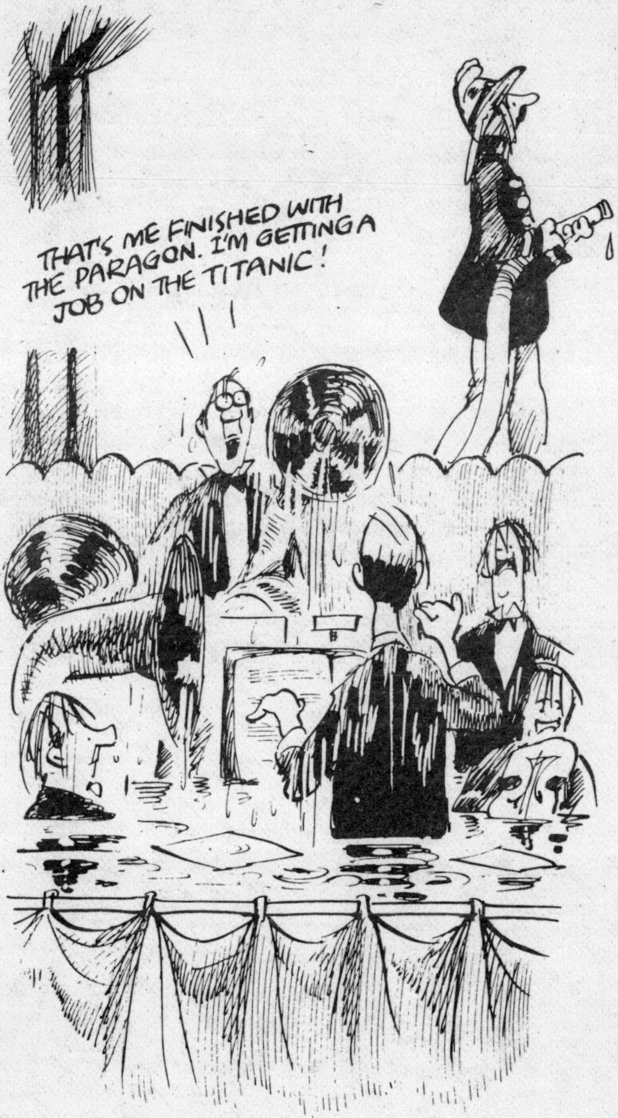
THAT'S ME FINISHED WITH THE PARAGON. I'M GETTING A JOB ON THE TITANIC!

WHEN GODIVA LOST HER BARINGS

Everyone was delighted when the sun shone on the big July parade at Lytham St Annes in 1983. But the star of the show, Lady Godiva played by sixteen-year-old Jane Austin, was nowhere to be found. She had left home and completely lost her bearings. As carnival organisers waited for two hours to start the parade, Jane, wearing only a body stocking, was struggling with a map astride her horse. Traffic police organised a search and found her three miles away, heading in the wrong direction towards the M55.

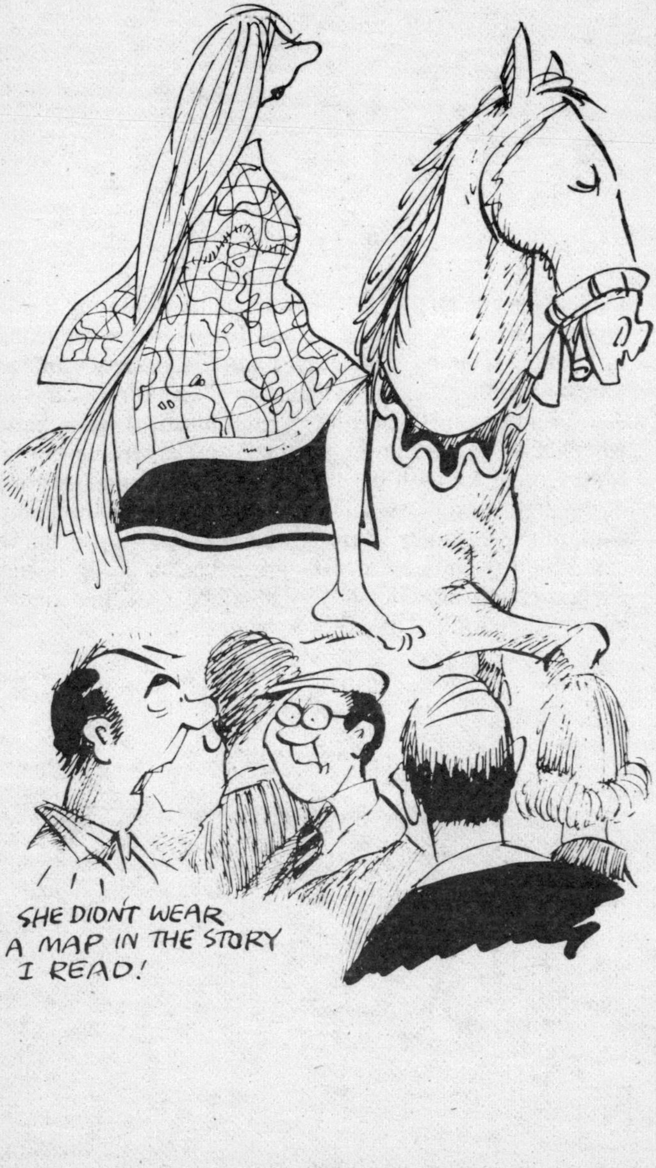
SHE DIDN'T WEAR
A MAP IN THE STORY
I READ!

REST CURE

Doncaster GP Dr Jan Lavric worked hard helping to take a party of disabled Catholics to Rome. When they lined up to be blessed by Pope John Paul, the good doctor sank thankfully into an empty wheelchair for a heaven-sent rest. A well-meaning Italian nun spotted him and immediately wheeled him, despite his protests, to the end of the line for an audience with the Pontiff. The Pope made the sign of the cross and blessed Dr Lavric, who rose to his feet to explain the mistake. There was a chorus of gasps from the assembled congregation. 'It's a miracle!' a group of nuns exclaimed. Dr Lavric said: 'The Pope read my identity badge, then looked at me in a strange way.'

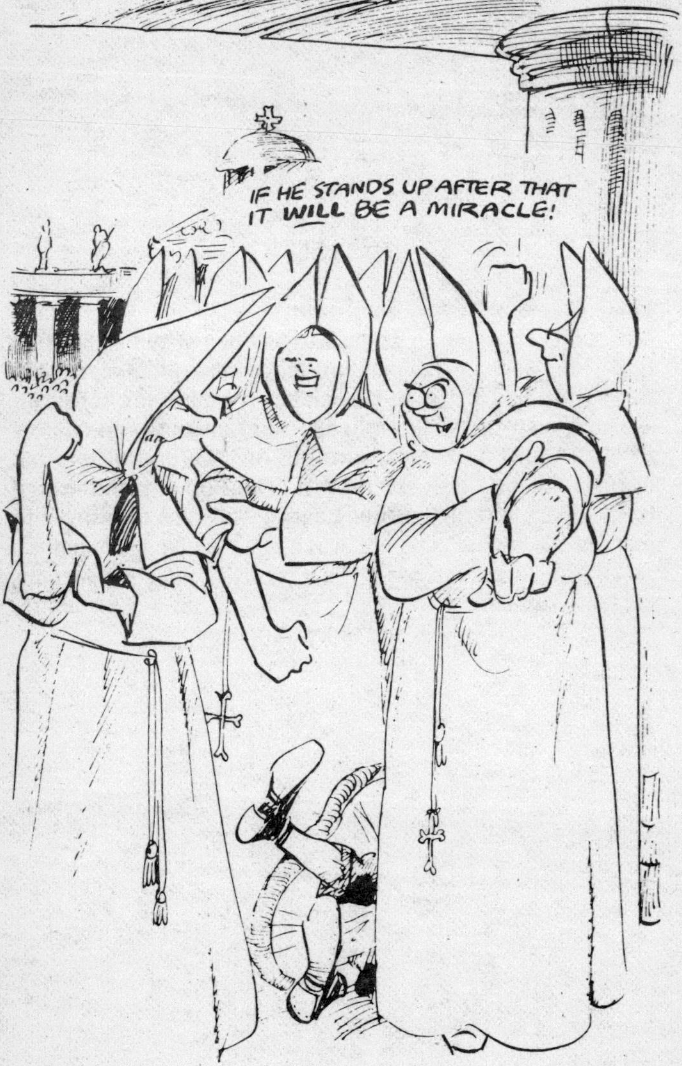
IF HE STANDS UP AFTER THAT IT WILL BE A MIRACLE!

MY HAT!

Mrs Frances Whalley, aged eighty-three, was just leaving her country cottage when she caught a whiff of smoke. Anxiously she checked the house, peering up the chimney and examining the plug sockets in every room, but to no avail. Wherever she went the smell of burning and haze of smoke became stronger, until she worriedly rang the fire brigade. When they arrived at her home in Leigh, Greater Manchester, firemen pointed out to Mrs Whalley that her hat was on fire.

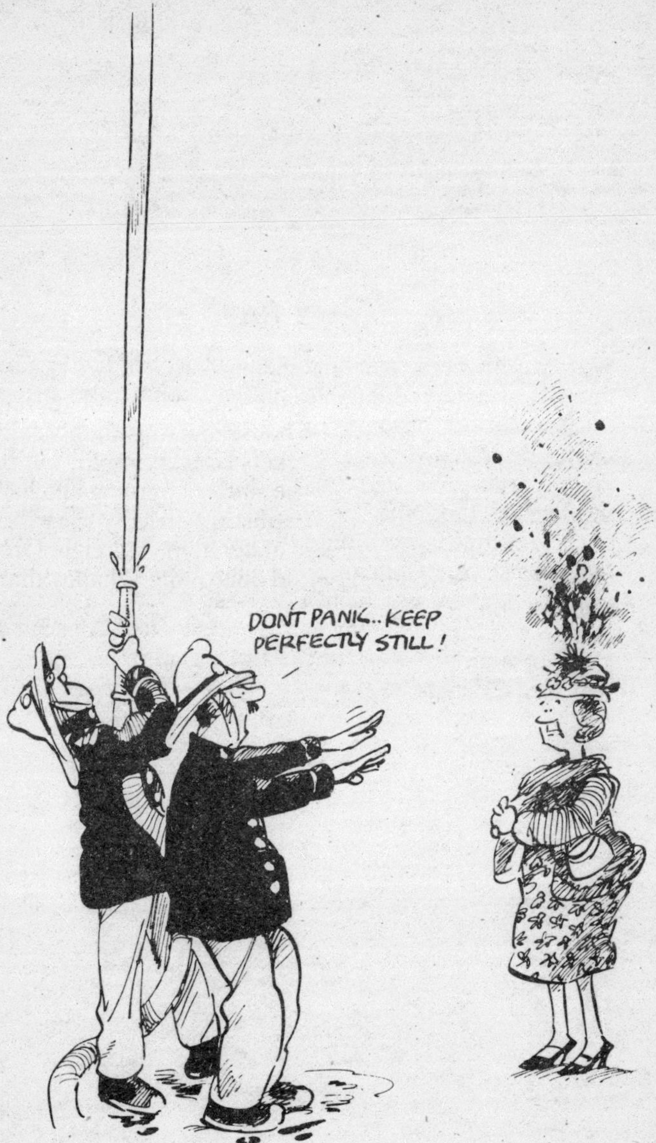
DON'T PANIC.. KEEP PERFECTLY STILL!

A CLOSE SHAVE

With his wife at the wheel of their car, Rotterdam engineer Peter Levy climbed into the caravan behind and stripped off to wash and shave. As they wound through the honking confusion of Barcelona's rush-hour traffic Mrs Levy's driving became more nervous and jerky. Then the traffic suddenly cleared and she put her foot down – catapulting her naked husband through the rear door of the caravan into the street. Clutching only his razor, he grabbed a cabbage leaf from a nearby vegetable stall for cover, as crowds gathered clapping and shouting '*Ole!*' Police finally bundled him into a patrol car and set off in pursuit of his wife and the caravan.

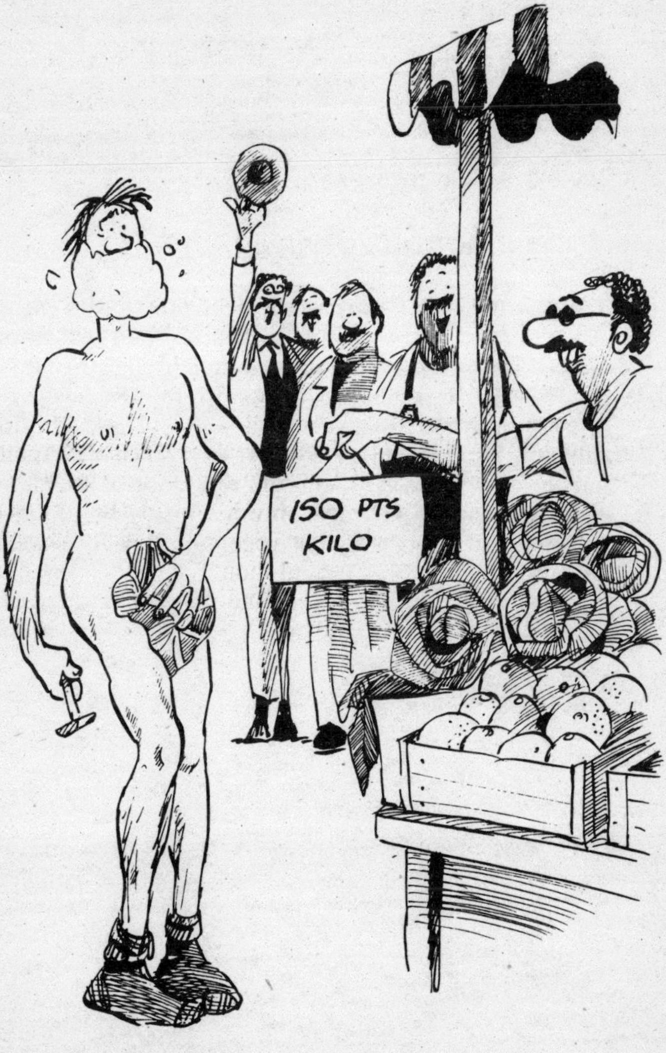
150 PTS
KILO

BLUE MURDER ON THE ORIENT EXPRESS

It was a mystery to tax even Hercule Poirot when the Orient Express refused to budge from Innsbruck station. Engineers made an exhaustive check, and even two specialists brought in could not solve the puzzle. Then staff began a wheel-by-wheel inspection to see if anything had jammed. Forty minutes later they discovered the reason. Behind the locked doors of a sleeping compartment, with the blinds tightly drawn, a couple were locked in heavy love-making – and the woman had her foot jammed against the emergency brake.

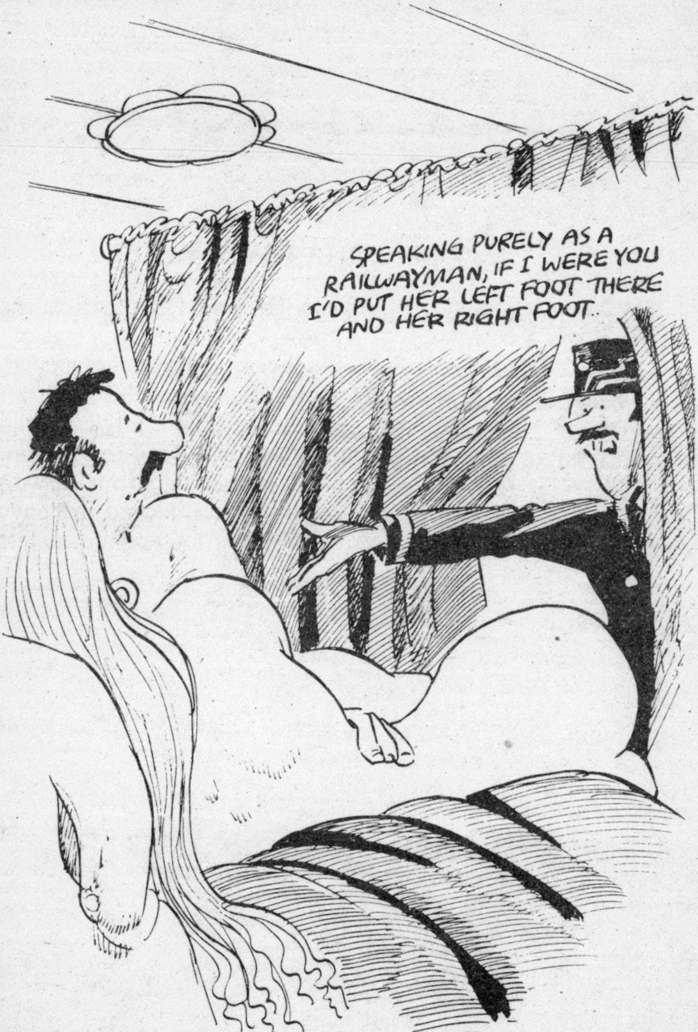
SPEAKING PURELY AS A RAILWAYMAN, IF I WERE YOU I'D PUT HER LEFT FOOT THERE AND HER RIGHT FOOT..

RAISING THE TOYTANIC

Modelmaker Brian Sandford toiled for ten years on his dreamboat – a superb scale model of the ill-fated *Titanic*. It was perfect right down to the last detail. Which is a pity – because it sank.

When Brian's big day came it was launched on a pond in Wimbledon where, like its namesake, it slid to the bottom on its maiden voyage. Divers eventually recovered it while Brian went back to the drawing board to design an unsinkable version.

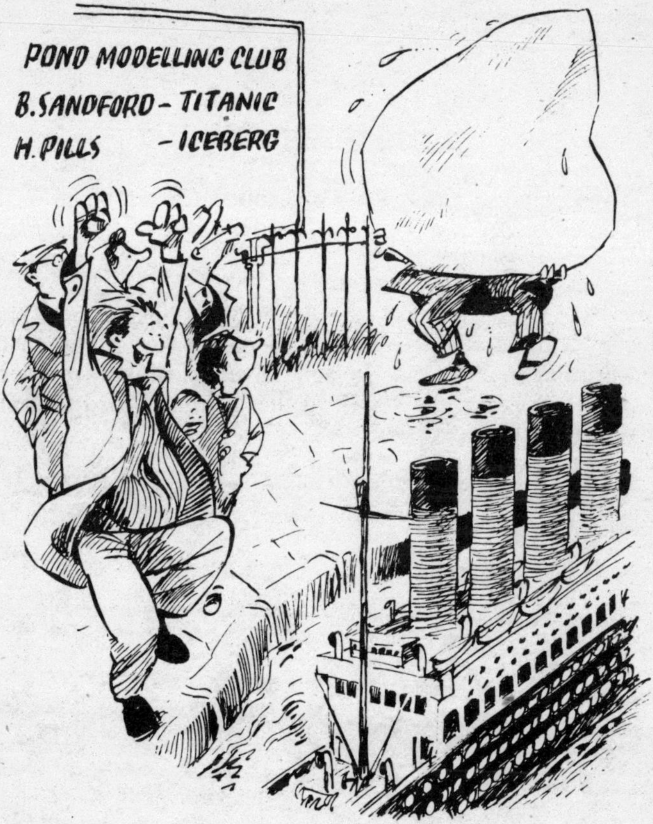
POND MODELLING CLUB
B.SANDFORD - TITANIC
H.PILLS - ICEBERG

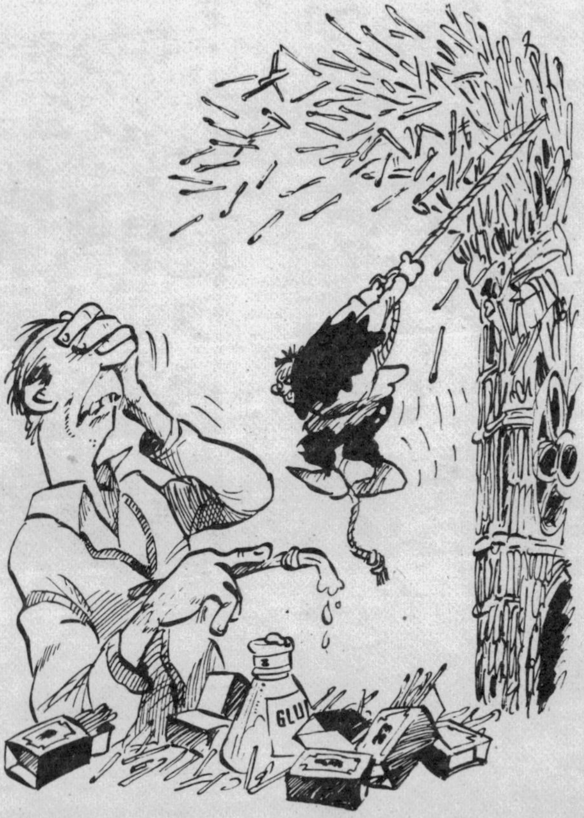
GLU